WINNING

in the Job Market

Mark Hempshell

TEACH YOURSELF BOOKS

Order queries: please contact Bookpoint Ltd, 39 Milton Park, Abingdon, Oxon OX14 4TD.
Telephone: (44) 01235 400414, Fax: (44) 01235 400454. Lines are open from 9.00–6.00,
Monday to Saturday, with a 24 hour message answering service.
Email address: orders@bookpoint.co.uk

A catalogue entry for this title is available from The British Library.

ISBN 0 340 72122 7

First published 1998
Impression number   10 9 8 7 6 5 4 3 2 1
Year   2004 2003 2002 2001 2000 1999 1998

Typeset by Transet Limited, Coventry, England.
Printed in Great Britain for Hodder & Stoughton Educational, a division of Hodder Headline
Plc, 338 Euston Road, London NW1 3BH by Cox & Wyman Ltd, Reading, Berkshire.

CONTENTS

INTRODUCTION: IT'S A JUNGLE OUT THERE!

Behind the smart offices and the neat industrial parks that are a feature of today's industrial and commercial scene is one single, simple fact: today's jobs market is a jungle.

For a start there are, in most cases, too many people seeking too few jobs. Employers themselves are under tremendous pressure to keep their businesses afloat and compete with other manufacturers and suppliers from around the world in the competitive global market which now exists. This filters through to employees who are themselves under tremendous pressure to meet deadlines, exceed targets, work harder and be more productive. Today, just holding down a job, let alone making progress in the jobs market, is an achievement in itself.

This means that when it comes to looking for a new or a better job or career you cannot leave anything to chance. You really do need all the help you can get. And the more advantages you can create for yourself – the more skills, experience, qualifications or talents you can muster – the better your chances of winning.

The jobs market of the future won't be a market of lifetime jobs, of nine-to-five type jobs, or of carefully planned careers. It will be a market of frequent job changing, flexible working, and the need to continuously adapt and retrain to meet the demands of the changing economy. Many employees already work in this sort of environment, and all the evidence suggests that in future more and more people will find that they need to be more and more flexible, and more and more competitive, if they are to survive in the employment market.

Of course, the changing jobs market is not all bad news. It often brings with it tremendous new opportunities. Such as the opportunity to learn new skills, work in new, more productive ways, gain greater seniority, gain greater control of your own career, and even earn more money. The kinds of opportunities that have always been available to the more privileged members of society will gradually become available to more and more ordinary people.

To exploit these opportunities you need information. Good information. The aim of this book is to bring you the information and advice that will help you through the jobs market jungle and show you how to take every advantage of the opportunities that the future holds.

Mark Hempshell

1 | WHAT JOB?: FINDING YOUR WINNING NICHE

The importance of knowing yourself

Do you want a job? Any job? The fact is, many people walk into any job as a means of providing themselves with an income, often without really thinking if the job is right for them. This is almost always a mistake. When you consider that you probably spend one-third of a typical day actually working, it underlines the fact that you really need to choose a type of work that you are very well suited to indeed.

Very few people would, for example, book a two week holiday or buy a car without thinking carefully whether it was right for them. So why choose a job or career in the same way? At least a two week holiday, badly chosen, is over in two weeks. If you choose the wrong job, however, you may have to spend a third of the rest of your working life doing it!

It is also true that the more you like your job the more easily you are likely to succeed in it. It is surprising how often the most successful people – business tycoons and multi-millionaires – spend every moment of the day working, and even work past retirement age when they could easily afford to retire – just because they enjoy their work so much.

Is it possible for the ordinary man or woman in the street to find him- or herself in this fortunate position? Almost certainly yes. But to achieve it you really have to know yourself, and know what you want from a job.

The following five leading questions should help you discover some useful information about yourself, and what exactly you want from a job:

■ *Given a free choice, what type of job would I like to do?* Answering this question honestly will give you a very accurate insight into the type of job that would be right for you. It might not be possible for you to do this job, for whatever reason, but there could be other jobs that involve the same sort of duties or projects.

■ *What types of things do I enjoy doing?* Think about the types of things that you enjoy doing out of work, including sports, hobbies or other interests. No one compels you to do to these things, so they must be things that really interest you. It might be possible to incorporate some of these things in your next job.

■ *What types of job would I definitely not want to do?* Given the very wide choice of jobs and careers on offer it can help to eliminate all those types of work that you definitely would not do. Rather than actual jobs as such think of the features of particular jobs that really wouldn't appeal to you. For example, do you dislike working alone, or working with figures? Do you like selling, or working outdoors?

■ *What outside commitments do you need to consider?* Traditionally employees were expected to devote themselves to their jobs regardless of other factors such as family commitments. This is an increasingly outdated idea and employers are now beginning to accept that work and family life must fit in together. In the modern jobs market it is becoming easier to balance work and other commitments.

■ *What outside pressures are there?* Most of us are under outside pressures from, for example, parents or partners, friends and colleagues to do a certain job in a certain way. Try to understand what pressures of this type you may be under, since pressures of this type are rarely helpful in finding the ideal job or career.

Has this given you a better idea of what you want to do? Hopefully yes, but throughout this book you will find a variety of advice to help you plan your career and win in the jobs market.

The personal audit

The personal audit is a good way of finding a job that is well matched to your personal skills, talents, qualifications, experience and other aptitudes and qualities. A personal audit is essentially a regular review of your personal situation in all those areas which affect your employability. Many of us use some of the principles of a personal audit on a random basis when thinking about our career. However, putting the personal audit on a more formal basis can make it much more useful and beneficial.

A personal audit normally concentrates on each of four personal aspects which affect our employability, which are:

■ Skills
■ Talents
■ Qualifications
■ Experience

To conduct a personal audit, examine each of these personal aspects and take some time to think about what they mean to you and how far they relate to the work you do.

Assessing your skills

A skill is considered to be a practised ability. That is, something you have learned or purposely developed. Skills can include:

■ *Physical skills:* Such as physical fitness or strength, or manual dexterity.

■ *Mental skills*: Such as mathematical skills, mental dexterity, wisdom, foresight, or a good academic education.

■ *Practical skills*: The ability to drive a vehicle, operate a certain machine, type or wordprocess, design or write.

■ *Personal skills*: By personal skills we mean qualities such as compassion, friendliness, warmth, the ability to deal with people or good organisational skills. Many possess these naturally to some extent but, normally, they are skills that have to be developed if they are to be useful. For example, you can't actually be a good organiser unless you spend a lot of time organising.

Assessing your talents

A talent is regarded as something that you have a special aptitude or faculty for. The difference between a skill or a talent is that it is generally accepted that you can't learn a talent. A talent may be a skill, but a skill isn't always a talent. Talents are often things that you feel you have what might be called a vocation or calling for or, often, things that other people have said they think you are particularly good at.

Here are some examples of talents:

■ Are you good at designing things, e.g. clothes?
■ Are you good at organising things, eg. events, meals?
■ Are you good at selling things?
■ Are you good at getting on with people?
■ Are you good at solving problems?
■ Are you good at negotiating?

Assessing your qualifications

Qualifications are some of the most important factors in getting a job nowadays and will become increasingly necessary in future. Employers not only expect their employees to know how to do something, but to be able to prove that they can learn how to do something and recall that knowledge at a later date. This is the main purpose of qualifications. Qualifications are also used as a bar or a filter to help in sorting applications. Hence it is often necessary to have a particular qualification for a particular job, even where that job does not involve the use of that qualification.

Qualifications can be awarded in two ways. Firstly, the main way, following a course of study which may be academic or vocational or both. Secondly, following completing a period of training or work. Both methods are increasingly valid.

The following list will serve as a guide when assessing what qualifications you have, or which you might want or need to obtain:

No qualifications

Unqualified is the lowest level on the jobs ladder. By unqualified we mean having no formal academic or vocational qualifications. This is increasingly unwise nowadays and restricts the opportunities on offer greatly. Anyone at this level should seriously consider how they can improve their level of qualification and, indeed, the increasing popularity of further education makes it easier than ever before to improve your qualifications.

School-leaving qualifications

As the job market becomes more competitive it is essential for all school leavers to ensure that they leave compulsory education with the highest level of school-leaving qualifications that their abilities will allow. Although the exact system in operation varies from country to country, in most countries the number of school leavers who go directly into the job market is decreasing. School qualifications should, therefore, be seen as less of a passport to a job but more of a passport to higher education.

Higher educational qualifications

Degrees: A degree is traditionally regarded as a qualification studied for at a university on a course normally lasting three years or more. All around the world this is an expanding area, with more students passing through higher education than ever before. As a consequence a degree is a prerequisite of entry to more types of career than ever before. Even in careers where a degree is not required as a condition of entry it is always a considerable advantage. Sometimes a degree is requested by employers not simply because it provides evidence of academic attainment but because it helps to control the number of applications for a particular job. In other words, it serves as a filter.

Degrees are becoming more vocational than in the past and many courses have moved away purely from academic learning to include a vocational element if not actual work experience. Graduates who have followed a course which includes a vocational element may find that they have an advantage when it comes to applying for a job.

In most countries degrees can now be more easily studied for by mature students during a break from work or even on a part-time basis. So, in the future more mature employees will find that they can benefit from studying for a degree and, similarly, that employers prefer those who can offer them whether or not they are directly relevant to the job in question.

Postgraduate studies: Postgraduate study remains a specialist area, and will probably continue to be so, bearing in mind the costs that are involved. Postgraduate studies are good preparation for an academic career but have increasing value in business, especially for senior management positions. Whereas in the past those holding postgraduate qualifications might have tended to follow an academic career they should find that an increasing number of career opportunities are open to them in commerce and industry. One example of a postgraduate qualification which has practical application in commerce and industry is the MBA which can now be studied for at universities and business schools around the world.

Vocational qualifications

A vocational qualification is any type of qualification which is intended as preparation for a job, hence the term vocation. Vocational qualifications cover a very wide spectrum, from qualifications awarded following a course of study at college, to qualifications awarded following a course of on-the-job training.

Vocational qualifications are perhaps the biggest and fastest growth area of qualifications and will become increasingly so in the future. They are used as qualifications enabling job entry by school leavers, and for more mature learners studying on-the-job or in part-time studies. They can be taken at the outset of your career, during your career, or even added to as you progress through your career. All employees should consider if and how they can benefit from improving their vocational qualifications.

Students at school and their parents should always ascertain what vocational qualifications may be available to them at school and school-leaving level since the systems in operation vary considerably from country to country. (In the UK NVQs or National Vocational Qualifications have now become one of the main vocational qualifications.) Aim to choose vocational qualifications that are portable and flexible. If you move to another employer, industry, or even a different type of work you will often find that the qualifications you have are still valid.

Find out about these qualifications from your employer or the professional association or training organisation which regulates your job or career area. Vocational qualifications may be offered by schools, higher education colleges and also by employers themselves. When offered by employers study for vocational qualifications can include on-the-job study, study at college, or a combination of both.

Other types of vocational qualification: Vocational qualifications are not necessarily only for school leavers and young people joining the workforce. Any type of qualification that helps you in work can be regarded as a vocational qualification. An evening class attended, a week-long training course, or a work-related seminar can all help you win in the job market. The best ones are those which are widely recognised and which provide written evidence of the qualification. The difficulty with some of these qualifications is that they are not widely known about, or not accepted by all employers.

Apprenticeships

An apprenticeship is best regarded as a combination of work and education. They are normally intended for school leavers, although they are also often available to those aged up to 19 or thereabouts. Where available, apprenticeships normally provide practical skills and education and a recognised qualification, often overseen by an industry training organisation or college. An apprenticeship is most suitable for those who want quality approved training but do not want to spend all or any of their time at college.

Other types of vocational qualification

Any type of qualification that helps you in work can be regarded as a vocational qualification. An evening class attended, a week-long training course, or a work-related seminar can all help you win in the jobs market.

The best ones are those which are widely recognised and which provide written evidence of the qualification. A difficulty with some of these qualifications can be that they are not widely known about, or not accepted by all employers.

Assessing your experience

Experience is becoming vitally important in the jobs market. It is a valuable asset, in many cases as or more valuable than even the best qualifications. Experience proves that you can do a job. It saves the employer having to train or retrain you, or wait for you to learn or develop the skills you need to do your job. It also shows that you can hold down a job and perform in the world of work on a day-to-day basis.

The question of experience has long placed many employees in something of a vicious circle – experience is difficult to come by, but you cannot be considered by many employers unless you have experience. This is likely to continue in future with all employers requiring experienced employees, but a limited number of employers actually able to provide it. All employees should regard building and developing their experience as very important indeed.

There are two types of experience, work experience and life experience.

Work experience

Work experience is, as the term suggests, experience of working. This is the most important type of experience you can offer to an employer. It shows, quite literally, that you can do the job.

Your experience does not necessarily have to be in the same job area as the one you are applying for. Employers appreciate any experience that shows you can function properly in a job.

When applying for jobs you should make use of all your experience. This includes full-time jobs but also part time jobs, contract jobs, voluntary work and even experience in a business.

Life experience

Life experience should be considered as a secondary type of useful experience compared with work experience. However, there are many experiences in life in general which provide you with experience that is useful in the world of work. For example:

■ Experience of holidays and trips abroad: this shows a knowledge of and openness to foreign cultures and unusual situations.

■ Experience of having children: this shows you are good at working with children and young people and (most parents would agree) good at dealing with stressful situations.

■ Experience of working on a committee: maybe you have experience of working as a local councillor, or on the fund raising committee of a local charity. This shows you can work well with others, plan and organise things.

The problem with experience is that it is not as easily documented as qualifications are. You must therefore aim to document it. Maintaining a good curriculum vitae (CV) is one way to do this, but also keep firm evidence of experience where possible such as testimonials and references and documents relating to projects you have worked on that have contributed to your experience.

The personal audit form

Once you have considered all these areas you may find it useful and helpful to actually write down what skills, experience, qualifications and other attributes you possess. This will help you best decide what qualities you can offer to an employer. It will also help you decide how these qualities can be developed.

A good way to do this is to copy and fill in the personal audit chart as illustrated in Figure 1.1. Repeat the exercise on a regular basis, such as every three or six months, to give you an idea of the progress you are making towards increasing your employability.

Exercises

1 Answer the five leading questions given at the beginning of this chapter. It may help to write your answers down.

2 Complete the personal audit chart, as set out in Figure 1.1.

3 Looking at, in turn, your *skills, talents, qualifications* and *experience,* consider what steps you could take over the next few months, if any, to enhance your prospects in each of these areas.

Once you have done this you can start to look at the opportunities which are available to you.

Name:
Date:

	Have now:	Working towards:	May have in future:
Skills (Include things you are good at. Things you like doing.)			
Talents (Include things that others say you are particularly good at.)			
Qualifications (Include all academic, vocational and non-vocational qualifications.)			
Experience (Include experience in life and in work.)			

Figure 1.1   Personal audit chart

How to choose the right industry

It becomes easier to choose a job or career on the basis of what type of industry it is located within. Rather than look at industries on the basis of what they produce, a more modern way to look at them is on the basis of what stage of development they are at.

Many experts consider all industries to be either sunrise, expanding or declining.

Sunrise industries

Sunrise industries is a term for new industries which have only started up within a relatively recent period and are not yet well established.

The advantages of working in them are that the range of job opportunities is increasing fast and high rates of pay are often offered to people with in-demand skills, qualifications and experience.

The disadvantages of working in them are that it can be difficult to get the skills, qualifications and experience you require in order to get these desirable jobs. The jobs are also changing fast and you need to ensure that you keep pace. Some sunrise industries can founder in the early years, leaving you with a skill that no one requires. Employers in these types of industries tend to start up, close down, go bankrupt or change ownership with remarkable regularity.

Some examples of sunrise industries are information technology, high technology manufacturing and many types of service businesses.

Expanding industries

Expanding industries can be described as industries which are expanding but which are already well established. That is, they are not sunrise industries. They are often connected with medium-tech areas rather than high-tech areas.

The advantages of working in them are that the range of job opportunities is growing and the industries are also secure. They are established and so less likely to founder than sunrise industries. They also often have skills shortages and offer attractive salaries to encourage people to join them.

The disadvantages of working in them are they are known to be expanding and so attract large numbers of job seekers, and depending on the job, competition for vacancies may be intense. There may also be intense competition for the best vacancies from extremely determined or so-called aggressive job seekers.

Some examples of expanding industries are transport and distribution, retailing and sales.

Declining industries

Declining industries are those which have ceased to expand and are reducing in size. This normally means that the number of job opportunities are actually reducing.

The advantages of working in them are few. However, in some cases, good jobs and attractive salaries are offered to those who are willing to work in them during the declining period. This can be worth considering so long as you have skills, experience and qualifications that are readily transferable to another industry. Some people consider a move abroad to a country where the industry is not in decline and where opportunities, salaries and conditions are often much better.

The disadvantages of working in them are chronic job insecurity. Your position may disappear at any moment. There is also often a stigma attached to those who work or have worked in these industries because they are seen as unfashionable, behind-the-times, and using outdated skills.

Some examples of declining industries are mining and many primary industries such as fishing and many areas of agriculture.

By considering at what stage of development the industry you choose is at you can see whether the opportunities are likely to be increasing or declining and this might help you make your decision.

Another way of looking at industries is:

Private sector

Private sector industries comprise businesses which are run by private individuals or companies for the purpose of making a profit. Their primary motive is profit. Although they may take customer service and employee welfare seriously this is not their primary aim.

The advantages of working in them are that they usually offer good pay and prospects. The disadvantages of working in them are that you may be under great pressure to meet performance targets. There is also an element of insecurity in that your job depends on the success of your employer.

Some examples of private sector industries in most countries are chemicals, the oil industry and motor manufacturing.

Public sector

Public sector industries are operations which are run by the government, local authorities or other official bodies. Their primary objective is not, if at all, making a profit. Their main aim is providing a service to the public. They may also have a role in managing the economy.

The advantages of working in them are that they usually offer secure employment and good employee benefits, in many cases providing lifetime employment. A disadvantage of working in them is that rates of pay are not always competitive with the commercial market. They may also involve learning skills which are not easily transferable to other employers or industries.

An example of a public sector industry in the UK is healthcare, although it is also partly within the private sector. Public sector industries are actually much more numerous in other countries where electricity companies, transport and distribution companies and airlines are frequently within the public sector.

Voluntary sector

The voluntary sector describes operations which are run on a not-for-profit basis, not by commercial businesses but also not by statutory authorities. A voluntary organisation is run for the public good.

Although much smaller than either the private or public sector the voluntary sector has an important and growing role. An advantage of working in voluntary organisations is that they offer interesting and rewarding jobs. The disadvantages of working in them are that pay and benefits are not always competitive with other sectors.

Some examples of voluntary sector organisations in the UK are the RSPCA, Oxfam and the NSPCC. Many of the UK-based voluntary sector organisations operate throughout the world, and the reverse is also true.

The trend towards mobility of labour

Mobility of labour is a situation where a worker or employer is not tied to a particular employer, industry or type of work throughout his or her career.

At one time, workers would enter a particular industry or type of work after leaving school or college and stay within that same field until retirement. Also traditional was a situation where jobs were handed down from father to son (rarely, however, from mother to daughter) thus keeping particular types of work within the family and restricting the choice of individuals.

This is true immobility of labour. It worked satisfactorily for many years when major, labour intensive industries were booming. However, this system has broken down and become ineffectual over recent years, because:

■ traditional heavy industries have declined in developed countries;

■ industries are developing at a frantic pace; and

■ we are now in a global economy.

It is generally unwise to be an immobile worker in the workforce. This could leave you stranded in a particular type of work when the demand for it has declined or even disappeared. A good example of an immobile workforce is mining in some countries. The industry has all but disappeared leaving many well qualified miners but no jobs for them to do, and with little chance of using those skills in any other industry.

The mobile workforce has skills which apply to many industries, thus:

■ making it easy to move from job to job; and

■ making it easy to move to more profitable areas of work.

To win in the workforce you therefore need to be as mobile as possible. That is, be able to work in as many different types of industry or work as possible. This done, you are unlikely to be short of work and can also move to booming areas with better rates of pay.

A good example of an immobile worker is a coal miner whose skills can only be used in the mining industry. But a good example of a mobile worker is a secretary, whose skills can be used in almost any business and who can move from employer to employer at will.

Here are some ways you can practise and benefit from the mobility of labour:

■ Learn skills that are transferable. That is, a skill that can be used in several different types of job.

■ Avoid learning skills that are not transferable, especially skills that are only useful in the actual job you do now.

■ Work for employers who are growing, especially those in sunrise industries.

■ Work for employers who are flexible.

■ Look for opportunities to do different types of work. For example, jobs that involve mixed and varied responsibilities.

■ Look for opportunities to expand your skills, whether by means of training courses or practical experience.

■ Look for extra training opportunities, especially ones that are documented.

How to choose the right type of position

One good way to choose the right type of position for you is to look at the level of skills that it involves. We are in a situation where skills relate to payment. In other words, the more skilled you are the more you will be paid, and also the more chance you have of moving to a higher skills level.

Generally it is always a good idea to enter or re-enter the jobs market at the highest skills level possible. It is also a good idea to seek to improve your skills level throughout your career.

Unskilled jobs

An unskilled job is considered to be one which can be done by anyone without any special skills or qualifications.

The advantages of this type of work are that it offers complete flexibility to acquire skills in whatever area you choose. You are not tied to one career and one area. Unskilled people are sometimes sought for training in new, sunrise industries.

The disadvantages of this type of work are that rates of pay, conditions and opportunities are often poor. Many employers are reluctant to hire unskilled workers at all.

In reality very few people who are entering or who are already within the jobs market are unskilled. Being unskilled is not the same as being unqualified and being unqualified is more of a problem to the jobseeker than being unskilled. If you lack formal qualifications then you should try to maximise your skills and promote these as being of value to employers. More job areas are falling within the semi-skilled or skilled categories.

Examples of unskilled jobs are cleaning operative and labourer.

Semi-skilled jobs

A semi-skilled job is regarded as any type of work which requires some skills or training to undertake the work. These are normally skills that are not achieved by formal study or training.

The advantages of this type of work are that you can receive extra pay for the skills that you can offer the employer. You may also be more employable. The disadvantages are that there are often many other people with this level of skills and others who can acquire them. Thus, there is often a great deal of competition for vacancies and other employees are able to move in on your skill at will. You may be out-skilled or even undercut by other employees entering the jobs market.

Examples of this type of work are semi-skilled jobs in factories, retail and some jobs within the catering industry.

Skilled jobs

A skilled job can be regarded as any job that requires definite vocational skills. In this regard we are talking about skills which are acquired following study on a formal course or training on a formal training course, normally, but not necessarily, which leads to the granting of a formal qualification.

The advantages of this type of work are that you have definite and recognisable job skills to offer an employer. You may also be occupied in an area of work which only skilled people can operate in, thus protecting employment opportunities.

The disadvantages are that, once you are engaged in this skill, it may be difficult to acquire other skills or develop existing skills. This makes it easy to fall behind in your level of skills training. It also makes it difficult to acquire new skills. It is particularly important for the skilled worker to ensure that they review and update their skills from time to time.

Examples of this type of work are tradespeople, factory machine operators, engineers, office workers with particular job skills, nurses and similar people.

Managerial jobs

A managerial position can be considered as any job which is organisational rather than functional.

The advantages of this type of work are that pay is normally higher where organisation rather than functional work is involved. There is also greater prestige, and a chance to access better opportunities.

The disadvantages of this type of work are that there is often great competition for the top vacancies within any one country. A tendency for downsizing and reduction of the levels of management means that there are fewer opportunities than in the past. Managers must also be skilled in a wider range of functions than was the case in the past when management hierarchies were much larger.

Examples of this type of work are bank manager, retail manager, and site manager.

All those who seek management positions should review their position and prospects from time to time. Middle managers are those most likely to experience challenges in the jobs market as the responsibilities of middle managers tend to be shared out between junior and senior management to reduce the cost of the management hierarchy.

Professional jobs

A professional job involves the type of work that requires a professional qualification. The advantage is that it usually leads to assured employment. Entry to the professions is strictly regulated by professional associations and usually pitched at a level that ensures full employment for all those who are accepted into the profession.

The disadvantages of this type of work are that it is extremely difficult to change to another type of work and impossible in many cases as professional qualifications are usually highly specialist. It is also difficult to accelerate the promotion structure beyond that which is set down.

Examples of this type of work include doctors and lawyers.

It is important to note that professional people are now very often required to possess skills in excess of their basic professional skills. For example, with some positions, doctors may be required to demonstrate financial acumen and good business sense as well as their essential clinical skills.

The trend towards multi-skilling

Multi-skilling is a situation where employees are able to do several jobs within a particular business or department rather than just one individual job.

A simple example of multi-skilling is working in a fast food restaurant, where each employee is able to prepare foodstuffs, cook main courses, prepare drinks, serve customers, clean and tidy the restaurant and even do administrative work, rather than each employee only doing one task. Fast food restaurants in fact were pioneers in the technique.

There are many advantages for employers using multi-skilling. It cuts training costs. It also cuts running costs, since staff can be scheduled more easily. At quiet times one member of staff can do the jobs of two. Multi-skilling was resisted by many trade unions but is now becoming common place.

Multi-skilling also benefits the employee. It allows you to gain more responsibility and offers more promotion choices. It also allows you to gain skills which can be used in other jobs. It is a good idea to become involved in multi-skilling wherever possible. Therefore:

■ Look for employers that operate multi-skilling when applying for jobs.
■ Put yourself forward for multi-skills training. This is normally to your advantage, as well as to the advantage of the employer.
■ If multi-skilling does not operate in your workplace then suggest it. Larger employers are usually aware of the concept, but many smaller employers are not.

However, here are a couple of points to watch about multi-skilling:

■ It may cross job descriptions. You may find yourself undertaking tasks which seem to be someone else's responsibility and which indeed were in the past.
■ It calls for flexibility and adaptability. Those who like to do the same tasks in exactly the same way need to change their outlook if they are to benefit from multi-skilling.

In the remainder of this chapter we will provide individual advice for those involved in particular sections of the jobs market.

Tips for school leavers

Over the last few decades the number of school leavers who have been moving from school directly to the world of employment has fallen sharply. Most school leavers now seek some kind of higher education or training before joining the workforce on a permanent basis. Jobseekers who choose to go directly to work shouldn't, however, see it as an easy option or shortcut. It may actually be more difficult to move into and progress through the jobs market from this starting point. The move from school to work is a big jump, which should not be underestimated. Here are some tips to bear in mind:

Leave at the highest level of qualifications. No matter what anyone says basic academic qualifications are always easier to obtain at school rather than later on in life. It is not always easy to get them later on nor is it cheap. If faced with a choice of going directly to a job or staying on to gain extra qualifications or improve those you already have then staying on is often the safest option.

Consider personal and practical skills as well as paper qualifications. No paper qualification, no matter how widely accepted or good it may be is a direct passport to the world of work. Your personal qualities and skills are also important. While many people have good qualifications far fewer have good qualifications and good personal qualities and skills and these can certainly tip the balance when looking for a job.

Think well ahead. The jobs market is changing fast. The jobs you are interested in now may be completely different or even completely unavailable when you leave school (or when you complete your higher education course). However, if you choose your job carefully there will always be other similar jobs to choose from.

Have an open mind. Consider as wide a range of jobs as possible, even those which at first seem of little interest. Don't suffer from 'career blindness' – a situation where you discover a job that you like the idea of and pursue it to the exclusion of all other opportunities.

Leave your options open. Remember there are thousands of different types of work out there. Situations can change completely. Your likes and dislikes can change completely. This often happens during your first year or two of work. Keep your options open by studying on courses or gaining experience that can be used in as many different jobs and careers as possible.

Make use of official channels of information. There are lots of different sources of information available to you and you should make use of all of them. This includes your school careers teacher or adviser and the local careers service. Never consider that they don't understand what you want, or that you don't need them. Even if you don't value their advice they are an access point to much other information and advice. Ask for an interview and any other information that you need.

Take care when taking the advice of well-meaning people. While it's always useful to have the advice of other people such as parents or friends do take care when following the advice. Remember, they won't have to follow this career path for the next 50 years or so – you will. The advice of impartial third parties such as teachers or a careers service is usually more objective. Even if you are determined not to do as they advise always consider the options that they suggest. There could just be something in them.

Don't be afraid to do your own research. Careers services and other sources of information try to keep tabs on every possible opportunity that is available to you but they can't always achieve this. The world of work and job descriptions are changing rapidly and information is liable to become out of date very rapidly. So, do your own research and go direct to the source wherever possible. Colleges and even employers are often very helpful, even if you are not joining the higher education world or the jobs market for some months or years ahead.

Exploit opportunities for further education and training. It's easy to consider that once you have left school you can stop learning. In today's jobs market this is rarely if ever true. Things are changing so quickly that in order to compete, and preferably stay ahead, you must continue to learn. This need not be within the classroom, it is more likely to be within the workplace. The added advantage is that you get paid to learn, unlike being at school.

Always look for employers who offer training and education opportunities. Always ask about them when applying for a job. Always ask about them when starting a job, and volunteer for them when available. Remember that training and education are expensive. If you take it on-the-job you can receive very expensive education and training at no cost to yourself.

Expect to change jobs. The concept of lifetime employment is disappearing rapidly. Industries and employers will need to be more flexible in future and won't be able to offer continuous employment as they battle to remain competitive. Never assume that jobs or industries which seem to be safe are safe. They could disappear within a few years. Hedge your bets by gaining skills, qualifications and experience that are applicable to many different industries.

Tips for students or graduates

Although the rise in those going into higher education is starting to slow down compared with the recent past the fact remains that anyone who has gone through some sort of higher education (defined as any course of study post-school) is always at an advantage. In some areas of work it has been the norm for many years. As such, it's important to manage your advantage in the right way.

Seasonal and regular fluctuations distort the picture. In some cases graduates are in short supply and eagerly snapped up by employers. In other cases there seem to be far too many graduates for the jobs and graduate unemployment rises. In all cases, however, remember that it is *always* an advantage. A majority of graduates earn higher than average salaries, usually much more.

Here are some tips to bear in mind:

Your education is valuable, market it wisely. A degree may have cost you, or your parents, a large amount of money. To an employer that qualification is worth many times more. In many ways, it comes as a bargain to them. So, while not wishing to appear arrogant, remember that you are offering them a very good deal by working for them.

Never see your qualifications as a passport to a job. A higher qualification should never be seen as a passport to a job. It is preparation for a passport to a job. Most employers consider it groundwork. A degree, for example, plus experience is usually a passport to a job.

Try to gain experience of the real world. One of the most frequent complaints of employers is that students become institutionalised and have very little (or no) experience of the world of work. Try to get an idea of the world of work, and also the commercial pressures that employers are under in today's competitive marketplace. Understand how difficult it is to run a business and make a profit. While placements and work experience are ideal anything that brings you into contact with the world of work is good, even part-time jobs and holiday jobs. Try to choose opportunities that get you involved with the business in question, rather than just use them as a source of income.

Don't neglect basic skills. No matter what a high level your course takes you to in your subject don't forget that basic skills are very important. These include skills like coherent writing, numerical ability, the ability to work as a team and delegate to others. They may be very basic skills but they are of great importance to employers.

Plan well in advance. Entering the world of work from higher education usually means that you are committing yourself to one direction of work or another. So, plan ahead as far as possible. Allow for the next five years, not just the next year. Also consider how the situation may have changed in ten or twenty years' time, difficult though it may be to think that far ahead.

Look at the jobs market as a whole. The market for graduates in any one year is pretty small. So, it makes sense to look at the entire jobs market and see where you can best fit into it. You may have planned to make a career in one area but things can change in three or four years. Are there other areas where the qualification you have (or hope to gain) can now be better used? Allow for flexibility and changes of plan.

Keep an eye on the trends. On the one hand it is important to keep an eye on the trends in the jobs market. This much is clear. However, you should also keep an eye on the trends that operate in the student (or, more accurately, graduate) jobs market. Look at expanding areas, declining areas, pay levels and requirements looked for by employers. Details about this can be obtained from the information published by professional organisations. Also read quality newspapers for information on trends.

Leave your options open wherever possible. Although you may be set on a particular career it is always wise to keep your options open as much as possible. Situations may have changed by the time your course is complete, and definitely by the time you reach the higher levels of your career area. In extreme cases, the job you wanted to do may have disappeared altogether. Keep your options open by choosing a course and elements within it that can be useful in several different areas of work.

Be practical. Don't loose touch with the reason for following your course – normally to find a job or career that you want to do rather than for the sake of studying. If your course is highly academic or theoretical in nature it is important to remain practical. Think of your course as a stepping stone not an end in itself. Employers almost always see things this way.

Think very long term. The course of study you are following may be to prepare you for a career lasting 40 years. Think how relevant your course will be in five, ten or twenty years' time, although it is very difficult to see this far ahead. What extra learning, skills or experience will you need to acquire to stay on top of things then? Choose a job or employer that will allow you to do this.

Always have a reserve in mind. One of the main difficulties encountered by students is choice of a career which later turns out to be unsuitable or, more usually, loses its appeal as it draws nearer. In extreme cases you may even be rejected for your chosen career, or the job may disappear altogether. To avoid this problem always have a reserve career in mind. If possible have several reserve careers in mind, ranked in order of priority, which can all be taken up following completion of the same course of study.

Keep an eye out for further training opportunities and additions to your skills. Never regard your course as a passport to a career in its own right. Even if it is (although this is rare), there may well be competition for the vacancies and so anything additional that you can offer an employer will be valuable. Look for further training courses additional to your course – such as a first aid course or an intensive language course. All these can help to tip the balance. Additional skills, such as dealing with people, organisation (gained from, for example, voluntary work or part-time jobs) can all make you a more employable package.

Consider the global employment market. The jobs market is becoming increasingly global. This most of all applies to well qualified and experienced people, especially students. It always pays to consider working abroad from the outset. You may find a wider range of career opportunities available in other countries and they may carry much better pay and conditions. Investigate the options from the outset. A period of work experience or a placement or exchange abroad might also be considered as a beneficial part of your course.

While it certainly makes sense to look at international opportunities from the outset it should also be noted that the best jobs abroad (the best choice of such vacancies) are available to those who not only have a good standard of qualifications but also those who have prior work experience, normally of at least two years.

Tips for the unemployed

Becoming unemployed will always be a difficult situation. The best advice here is to consider that it is not unemployment that is the chief problem, but re-employment. Focus your efforts on finding a new position, rather than coping with the last position.

One consolation is that becoming unemployed and periods of unemployment will become more common place in future. As a result it is likely to become less of a stigma. There is also likely to be more help available for the unemployed. At the end of the day, however, self-help is the best course of action to adopt.

However, here are some tips to help you:

Start the new job search immediately unemployment becomes likely. It's much easier to find another job from the position of being employed, even in a job with no future. So, assuming you have some notice start the new job search the very day you find out. If you find the job you want right away don't be afraid to leave your last position. After all, your last employer owes you nothing.

Recognise that being unemployed when applying for a job is a distinct disadvantage. Address the difficulties rather than ignoring them.

Make use of help and advice offered by your last employer. You may not feel disposed towards accepting help, but it can be valuable. If help is not offered ask for it. Suggest your employer pays for help from a professional redundancy adviser.

Make use of local authority and government help. There are lots of sources of official help. Check them out. Make a list of everything that is available and then work through obtaining the assistance to which you are entitled. Look at such areas as the national employment service, social security offices, training and enterprise companies and economic development services run by local authorities. Be determined. Many of these services are under great pressure and will only give help (or give their best help) to those who are most persistent. Find out what you are entitled to and then follow it up.

But don't rely on help from other sources. At the end of the day it is still the individual who is responsible for finding and maintaining a job. This is never likely to change. No matter what help you are offered from, for example, a national employment service, always see this as a supplement to the help you provide to yourself.

Try to occupy your time productively. Try and use the time while you aren't working to do something that can actually improve your employment prospects. For example, take a course, do voluntary work, start to learn a language, try a new hobby and so on. Try to choose things that are job- or work-related. If these activities don't benefit you now they will at some time in the future. There are lots of things you can do that won't affect any social security benefits you might be entitled to and your unemployed status might even mean you can do them much more cheaply than normal, or possibly even free of charge.

Treat job hunting as a full-time job. It's useful to treat looking for a job with the same importance as a full-time job. Allocate some time to it each and every day – and organise it in the same way you would your work. This doesn't mean you have to work at finding work Monday–Friday, 9am–5pm (remember a decreasing number of jobs work this way), but do work on it daily – and do take time off at the weekends.

Don't rely too heavily on your past experience. While it's true that employers like to see evidence of good past work experience you shouldn't rely too heavily on this. It's a good recommendation for you, not a passport to a job. If anything, experience you have gained within the last one or two years is most valuable. Experience gained even five years ago may be out of date and experience gained ten years ago may even be totally irrelevant.

Polish up on your skills and qualifications. The time you become unemployed is a good time to check up on your skills and qualifications if you haven't done so already. Are they still relevant to the world of work? Do they need to be updated? What deficiencies are there between the skills and qualifications that job seekers who are newly entering the market have? Look at opportunities for updating them, either through a college course or a method such as voluntary work or a part-time job.

Use every possible source of jobs. It's very important to realise that no single source of job vacancies can be relied on. Many employers never use the national employment service. Some employers only use private employment agencies. Some employers routinely advertise every vacancy. Many employers never advertise vacancies and recruit from the people who contact them. Make a list of all the methods you could use and combine them all, even those methods which you have never used before. And even consider new methods, such as the Internet.

Be willing to try totally new directions. Expert opinions are divided as to whether those who become unemployed should keep looking for a job of the same type as their last employment, or look for a totally new direction. Probably the best advice is that you should at least consider new directions, even if you do not actually take them.

Be willing to start at a lower position on the career ladder. This is a clever technique used by some unemployed job seekers. It relies on the fact that in most types of work there are fewer vacancies at each level the higher you move up the promotional hierarchy. Thus, by taking a step (or two) down the ladder you should find many more opportunities on offer to you. In most cases this shouldn't be a problem because, if you really were capable of operating at your previous level, you should quickly be able to move up within the structure. This can often be more effective than waiting longer for a job at your previous position on the career ladder.

Consider part-time, temporary or contract positions as a half way house on the road back to full-time employment. It is usually much easier to secure a permanent job, and the type of job you wish to do, from a position of being partly employed, or employed in a type of work other than that which you are looking for, than from the standpoint of being completely out of work.

Don't consider self-employment if you wouldn't have started your own business anyway. Self-employment offers tremendous opportunities – but only if it's what you want to do. If you see self-employment as second best then it will always remain so. If you feel that you are a born employee then it is much better to remain one.

Tips for returners

Returners can best be described as those people who have past experience of the world of work but who have been absent for a time before returning to the jobs market. Returning used to be considered a minority activity. Today, however, it is becoming more usual if not exactly common place. In particular, the typical returner is no longer necessarily a woman, returning to work after bringing up children. She, or he, may well be a more mature individual, returning to work after retirement, or an individual of any age returning to work after a period of illness or voluntary absence from the job market.

So, here are some tips to help the returner:

First, try not to lose contact completely, thus avoiding the need to return. Could you work part time, a fraction of time, or fill in for holidays and absences?

Recognise that work returners are at a disadvantage from day one. It doesn't matter how normal your period away from work has been, it may still be considered abnormal by some – even to have children. You'll be considered out of touch and outskilled. Rather than pretend that these barriers don't exist do everything possible to combat them.

Do your homework. Find out if and how far you are behind current practice. Returners tend to find they are not as far behind as they expect. Finding you're not that far behind can be a big confidence boost. Chat with friends and colleagues about their jobs and see how much you need to come up to speed on current practice.

Make use of assistance schemes. Take advantage of any government or other schemes or assistance that might be available, even if you think it doesn't apply to you.

Do what you can to brush up on your skills and qualifications. Even if they're seemingly minor things it shows a positive attitude to returning to the world of work.

As a first step, consider part-time work. Consider a part-time or temporary job as a stepping stone to the world of work

Apply to companies that positively welcome returners, rather than see it as a disadvantage. In the case of big companies you can often find out what their policy is by asking their head office.

Look for jobs where your time out can serve as a positive contribution to the company you work for, rather than a barrier.

Once you start your new job do a quick assessment to find out how far you're out of touch. Devise a quick action plan to bring you back to full speed as quickly as possible. Find out about any training or courses that may be available. If these relate directly to your work your new employer may be willing to pay for them.

How to change your career direction

Changing your career direction or, in other words, moving from one type of work to a completely different type of work, has always been a rather unusual process and considered that way by employers and other people in the workplace. As such, it was a difficult process, hampered by the prejudices of others as well as practical problems.

At the moment, although career-changing is by no means common, there is evidence that it is becoming more accepted. This has mainly come about because of the pressures of the marketplace and the changing structure of industry and commerce rather than because it suits employees. As such it is likely to become easier in the future, although still something that requires careful consideration and planning.

Here are some tips if you are considering changing career direction:

Get as much information as possible. Find out everything there is to find out about your proposed career change. Obtain as much information as possible about your new line of work. If possible, talk to someone who works in that job. If possible (although it's often not possible) talk to someone who has changed from your job to the job you intend to move to.

Get the decision right first time. Changing your career once can be tricky. Changing it twice can be a major headache. Don't change careers just to see what it's like. It can also be very difficult to change back to your original career if things don't work out as employers will wonder why, and you may even fall behind with current practice in that industry.

Recognise that things have certainly changed since you started your first career. The jobseeking process may be easier. Or it may be more difficult. Recruitment almost certainly isn't handled in the same way.

Consider the age element. It is certainly a problem. There is still a degree of prejudice amongst employers and fellow employees against people who change careers, especially later in life. Remember that most recruitment and induction systems are orientated towards younger people, especially those who have no previous work experience. Try to look for employers who don't see age as a barrier or, alternatively, make sure that you are willing to start at the bottom and deal with the difficulties of starting way down the career ladder – again.

Avoid the so-called 'grass is always greener syndrome'. That new job you have your eye on may not be as exciting and well paid as you imagine. In fact, many people who do it would probably gladly swap for your job.

Recognise the difference between a forced change and a change of choice. You may be forced to change your career if, for example, your employer goes out of business or you are working in a declining industry. In all other cases your change is a change of choice. This gives you many more options. In these cases take a longer time to make the change, rather than a shorter one.

Look at a transition rather than a complete break. Explore ways that you could make the move from one industry to another gradually, rather than all at once. This will give you extra time to adjust and will also give you the opportunity to stop and/or backtrack if you wish. Look for other job areas that use some of the skills you use in your current job and some of the skills you will need in your new choice of career.

Look at how your qualifications and experience can be re-used in your new job. This avoids having to start again at the bottom. Audit your qualifications and experience and see what elements of them apply to other types of work, without any further retraining. Identify key elements that are the same, so that you can take these points up with employers when applying for new jobs. This is particularly easy with unitary qualifications, where core and key skills units may be identical in what otherwise appear to be totally different jobs. It is more difficult to make these comparisons with, for example, a degree but it can be done. You may find that you are more qualified for the changed career area than you expected.

Look at how your qualifications can be re-used, perhaps with moderate updating. One of the great difficulties of changing careers is that you may need to start again with completely new qualifications, which can take time, cost money and keep you away from the world of work while you retrain. Instead, look at ways of adapting or updating those qualifications, such as on short or intensive courses. Alternatively look at opportunities for part-time study, especially part-time study sponsored by your employer, such as day release programmes.

If possible, prepare for your new career before you make the change. Look for extra experience you can gather, or extra training you could undergo. You may even be able to obtain this courtesy of your current employer.

Concentrate on industries which have an established track record of recruiting job-changers. These tend to be newer industries which are expanding faster and which can't find sufficient people who are completely new to the industry. For example, ten years ago the computer industry recruited exclusively job changers since there weren't enough (or any) suitable school and college leavers to fill new posts.

Apply to employers who are more than willing to accept career-changers and who see it as an advantage. However, these tend to be career areas which other people leave also for a change of career, perhaps because they have become disillusioned by it. Nursing is a case in point here.

Tips for mature job changers

While it is true that employers do tend to favour younger people this is not always the case. As the population in many countries matures, employers will be forced to look at older people more seriously. This assumes, of course, that they do not do so already and the situation is not as bleak as it may seem from the situation of looking for a job.

There is generally no reason why mature job seekers cannot be employed in modern industries and modern practices if they have the necessary skills, experience and qualifications. Broadly, there are very few areas that are a 'young man's (or woman's) job'. The impression that some jobs are only for young people is media hype and not often true in practice. Although it's not always easy there are plenty of mature people working in sunrise industries. But you must keep up with current trends.

Here are some tips for mature job changers:

See maturity as a problem, at least in the short and medium term, until attitudes change. To be older is seen as a disadvantage by most employers so treat it as such and try to combat it, rather than choosing to ignore it. Yes, you have years of experience and it should count for something, but often it is better to just accept that unfortunately it doesn't count for as much as you think.

Try to keep an eye on current trends. It's hard to underestimate just how quickly the business and industrial scene is changing. Think back to when you last felt your knowledge of your particular type of work was state of the art. Was it five years ago? Ten years ago? Try to find out how what you do has changed, when considering modern practice.

Update your skills as much as possible. Perform a skills audit and see how far your skills are behind current practice. Are they a short step or a giant leap? It's normally not as difficult to update them as you might imagine. Look at skills training that is available on government schemes and with new employers. Colleges of further education are also very often helpful and nowadays welcome applications from mature students. In some cases they positively encourage them.

Never believe that you can't operate in the modern world. The differences are often not as great as you think. You may often lack modern skills but these can be learned, if you have the right attitude of mind. Basic skills like numeracy, good communication skills, good people skills and so on remain the same throughout the years and, as a mature jobseeker, you probably possess these skills in abundance. They are also the skills that younger job applicants very often lack.

Embrace modern technology. In most cases it's not the demon that you might think it is. A case in point here is computer technology. In many cases its easier for mature people to learn state-of-the-art techniques since they are not hindered by the continuous changes in technology that other people have had to cope with as computing has developed over the last few years. It's relatively easy to learn these new skills by part- or full-time courses and computer training.

Stand on your track record. Think about your achievements, get them documented and present them to future employers. Don't go too far back however. A small achievement within the last five (or at most ten years) is much better than a massive achievement 20 or 30 years ago.

Aim for the types of job that suit mature people better. Despite what we have said in this section there is often bias against older people by employers or colleagues who think that older people can't do the job. So, you stand a much better chance of re-entering the jobs market, if only as a first step, with a type of job that suits mature people better. Types of jobs that this applies to includes jobs that involve good people skills, listening skills, counselling skills and similar qualities.

Apply to companies who welcome mature applicants. You can normally find out what policy is on this matter by contacting head office. A number of companies, major and minor, are actually biased towards mature applicants and will usually be pleased to tell you about this policy.

Tips for disabled job seekers

Disabled job seekers face particular problems when seeking work. The situation is not especially easy but all the signs are that it will improve in future, if slowly. On the one hand legislation should become more comprehensive and more evenly applied. However, economic considerations are probably most helpful of all. Skill shortages will mean that well skilled and qualified people, even if disabled, will become more and more in demand.

Here are some tips for disabled job seekers:

If choosing a career (or changing direction or returning) choose an area of work which currently has skills shortages and seek training in those skills. This will make you more sought after and give you a better choice of opportunities at better rates of pay.

Identify your strengths and look for work areas that can use those. It is even better if they are areas where you can compete or even beat able bodied people. For example, if you are physically disabled but are excellent at dealing with people by telephone look for those types of jobs.

Devise routes round your weaknesses. For example, if you work in sales but are unable to travel easily look for a job in telesales or internal sales and make that your speciality.

Specialise in something, so that your disability pales into insignificance compared to your specialist skills or knowledge. Look for training and entry opportunities in sunrise industries where the skills you will learn are likely to be in short supply and employers may well be forced to recruit well-qualified applicants regardless of disability.

Make use of any governmental, local authority or voluntary organisation schemes that are available.

Look for employers that are not only willing to recruit disabled people but are positive about it. Ask employers about their policy on this. Also ask voluntary organisations that you may be in touch with to tell you about positive employers.

Look at the practicalities in advance. Investigate the place you will work. Recognise that few employers are able or willing to make special provision for, for example, disabled access unless or until they are forced to. However, provision of good access and other facilities is sometimes a sign of a positive attitude towards recruiting disabled people. It is always a good indicator that the employer can't rely on practicalities like this as a means of discriminating against you throughout the application process.

Be ready for problems and discrimination in the recruitment process. Have answers ready for the likely questions about the problems that may be caused.

Consider alternative options, such as self-employment, contract work, homeworking and teleworking. These often put you on a more level playing field in comparison with able bodied workers and also make it easier for employers to utilise your skills. In the extreme, high technology methods of working can even give you a positive advantage over other workers when properly deployed.

Expose discriminatory employers. Publicity can encourage them to change their policy, although it may not persuade them to employ you!

Tips for ethnic minorities

While all the tips in this book apply to all job seekers it may be useful to consider some special points. Ethnic minorities have always had problems in the job market and these are unlikely to be solved easily in future. However, since skilled and qualified people will be more in demand in future skilled and qualified ethnic minorities *are* likely to find that they are not only more employable, but more keenly sought than ever before.

Recognise that discrimination exists even where there is a stated policy to the contrary. Even employers and bosses from ethnic minorities can practise discrimination.

Realise that whatever the law says not all employers are enlightened, nor are they ever likely to be. It is much better to try to fit in with the system as it exists rather than sit around waiting for a perfect world, or for that perfect job to appear. By then you'll already be moving up the career ladder and, in addition, be in a much better position to change things – from within rather than from outside.

Aim not to make use of positive discrimination wherever possible. Seek a job on your own merits. Opportunities which offer access through positive discrimination are often very limited in depth and breadth, no matter how well intended they are. You may find that there are very few opportunities for promotion and development.

It is much better to look for employers who willingly recruit ethnic minorities wherever possible. It is not enough merely for employers to say that they are willing to recruit ethnic minorities. Look for employers who actually do it and offer them the full range of training and development opportunities.

Look for jobs where your special skills and talents are useful or even positive requested. Examples include the ability to speak languages or work well with your community. These are valuable assets and it is a great pity not to take advantage of them.

Skills and qualifications are particularly important. If you are well skilled and qualified potential employers will find it much harder to turn you down for any job.

Extra skills and talents are always a good way of gaining an advantage over other applicants. They represent added financial value as to why an employer should recruit you – and few employers will turn down the financial advantage of extra skills for no (or little) additional salary.

Recognise that discrimination is covert as well as overt. Problems such as glass ceilings and nepotism operate as much if not more by some employers even if you are awarded the job.

As a last resort, expose discriminatory employers. Bad publicity can work wonders in encouraging them to change their policy.

How to get further help

The aim of this chapter has been to serve as a method of self-counselling. However, you may need extra help. Here are some sources:

School careers services

School or college careers services are the first step on the careers guidance ladder. They are the only form of advice that is specially designed and equipped to assist those who have no experience of the world of work. As such they are a good source of advice. They do, however, have a tendency to see things quite narrowly, based on past experience or the area they are situated in. In the global economy it is best to take a wider view.

Here is how to get the best from such services:

- *Take up your entitlement to free careers guidance*. Insist on an interview.
- *Go prepared to your interview with ideas of what you want to do and some basic information about them*. To do this, use the library, and ask friends and colleagues.
- *Listen to the basic advice*. It is based on a lot of experience. Even if the interviewer (who may be one of your teachers) seems to know nothing they almost certainly have something valuable to contribute.
- *Don't be swayed into things that you don't want to do*. However, do be prepared to consider other options that are suggested to you, even if they are of no interest at the time.
- *Exploit special events*. Example are careers fairs, open days and trips to colleges or employers.
- *Do your own further research*. Careers services try hard to know everything about everything but it's almost impossible, especially with budgetary restrictions. Find out things for yourself. Write to employers and training organisations. Read newspapers and books.
- *Try not to be influenced by friends*. They almost certainly don't share your career interests.

University careers services

Some people may feel it is a little late to be choosing careers once you are at college but this is rarely the case. Remember that a degree, for example, is still a very general qualification and can have many possible uses. You may have set your mind on a particular career when you started your course of study but you are sure to find out that there are many more choices.

- *Be ready to change your mind*. It is perfectly realistic. You do not have to be locked into a career linked to a course of study which you might have chosen up to five years ago.
- *Make use of university careers services*. You're not expected to have made all the decisions nor to be able to do everything by yourself even towards the end of your course. Don't hesitate to ask for help or information. Remember that they have experience of thousands of similar situations to yours and know the best course of action, the shortcuts and the pitfalls.
- *Be open to other options, especially if your original choice of career has become more restricted*. If necessary don't be afraid to consider

changing or restructuring your course (where practical) to accommodate a change in career direction. No matter how hard it may seem to change now, it is a much better time to change than several years into the world of work.

■ *Ask what special links your careers service or your departments can arrange*. For example, meetings with employers, work experience and other links, such as placements and exchanges

Making use of recruitment drives

The annual recruitment drives by major employers can still be of tremendous use, but you must exploit them properly. Although in recent years we have seen fewer employers participate in these events it is likely that they will again become more important as employment opportunities rise and graduates become in greater demand yet again.

Remember that the employers represented are only representative of the jobs market. They are mainly national companies, or large local employers. Thousands of career opportunities are rarely represented at these events.

The employers are most definitely out to recruit you. It is an incredibly cheap way of recruiting high calibre personnel of the future for them. This does not mean they are right for you. Be objective no matter how impressive their claims, offers and promises.

If in doubt accept an offer, but make sure you can back out later. Make sure you understand the day-to-day realities of working for this employer.

The main benefit of events like this is the opportunity to mix with 'real live' people who work in industry. Benefit from their experience. Could you see yourself working with them and, if not, who would you like to work with?

Your current employer

Never believe that your current employer cannot help you with your career. They often can and it is one of the few ways of developing your career which is available free. It also shows your interest in developing your career and may help to put you in line for promotion opportunities.

■ *Check to see if there are any official counselling or advisory services*. Larger employers often have these or are willing to provide them.

■ *Check to see what help is available with career development from the personnel department.*

■ *See if there is a newsletter or bulletin describing opportunities in other parts of the organisation.* This is often the case with large employers, government departments or local authorities. Find out if there is a single person you can contact to discuss applying for these positions.

■ *Find out what personnel skills development courses may be on offer to you.* These may be primarily intended to help you with your work for this employer but the skills can be used equally in any employer. Courses conducted by outside agencies are particularly valuable in this respect.

■ *See if your employer will pay for outside assistance.* This is more likely the case with smaller companies who don't have internal facilities.

Government and local authority initiatives

Helping people with their careers is important to governments and local authorities. It reduces unemployment, brings extra money to their areas, and of course extra income by way of rates and taxes. Always look to see what schemes there are that you could take advantage of as they are almost always free.

■ *Ask your national employment service (where available).* They know of some, but not all, schemes.

■ *Ask at your local library.* They will have leaflets, directories and may have access to electronic databases or Internet resources.

■ *Ask your employer.* They are sometimes involved with schemes, especially where voluntary redundancy or downsizing is involved.

■ *Look out for television and press advertising.* Some schemes apply only to local and regional areas and may not be promoted nationwide.

Voluntary organisations

Voluntary organisations are not often thought of as sources of career help but a surprising amount of help is available this way. Several voluntary or charitable organisations have made career development and advice their interest. Some of these work for the community at large whereas others work for specific groups, such as women's or ethnic groups.

It is worth looking at how you can take advantage of this help. Some of these services are undersubscribed because few people know about them. The quality of their assistance, which includes information, practical help and financial help is usually very good.

- Ask your national employment service (although they often do not know much about these services).
- Ask at your local library.
- Ask your local authority.
- Look in directories, such as *The Voluntary Agencies Directory*, to see if there are any agencies which can help you.

Commercial counselling services

Commercial counselling services are companies which provide careers advice and guidance as a business. They normally charge a fee direct to the employee or jobseeker, although costs are sometimes covered by employers.

Commercial career counselling organisations are a growing industry, even though the fees are by no means low. More people are willing to pay for good quality advice. Generally the service is more personal and detailed than that provided by free services.

Commercial services operate at two levels. Firstly, it is provided to children of school age whose parents are willing to pay for individual advice. Secondly, it is provided to executives, normally with several years' experience, and particularly in the later stages of their careers. In this case the counselling service may also be able to provide employment leads, or place clients into positions which they are retained to fill. This service is not offered by all counsellors however.

Here are some tips on getting the best from commercial career counselling services:

- Only use a commercial service if you have an open mind about your future career path. If you are set on taking a certain route then there is little point in consulting a counsellor as you are very unlikely to take their advice.
- Use a long established service if at all possible.
- Use a service that is recommended to you by others, or which you are referred to.

■ Ask for examples of people they have helped to give you some idea of exactly what they have done.

■ Give them full and complete details of, for example, your past experience and qualifications.

■ Make use of referrals that they can arrange and contacts with employers and other organisations.

Commercial counselling services cannot really be considered as offering a quick fix, nor should they be used by those who expect a quick return on their investment. They are most useful to those who are willing and able to invest a little time and money now in the expectation of being further up the career ladder in, perhaps, ten or twenty years' time.

Summary

■ Always be aware of what you can offer to the jobs market. Be aware of exactly what skills, experience, qualifications and so on you can offer and how they can be improved.

■ Make use of a periodic personal audit.

■ Keep informed about how employers and their industries are changing and developing. Consider from time to time if and how you should be changing too.

■ Be aware of the special difficulties or opportunities that might apply to your particular situation.

2 | WINNING BY IMPROVING YOUR MARKETABILITY

Marketability: the buzzword

Marketability is very much a buzzword for all those seeking to find or change jobs. What exactly do we mean by the term marketability?

The best way to think of this is to put yourself in the position of a company producing a product or selling a service. To produce their product they take many component parts and bring them together and assemble them in a product. It may be chemicals, raw foodstuffs, electronic components or whatever. All of them go into producing the final product.

One important component in that product are the people who make or sell it. They are just as important as all the other component parts involved in the process. In fact, today, they are more important. With manufacturers and service companies all providing much the same end product the difference in the service they provide is very often what differentiates them from other producers and, most importantly of all, one of the things that brings customers to their door.

When producing their product the company have many choices as to the suppliers they use. They can shop around and find the best source of chemicals or packaging, or the best supplier to deliver their goods for them. They can also shop around and choose the best people to use in their business.

When you make yourself marketable you make yourself as employable as possible. By marketability we mean acquiring as many skills, qualifications, developing as many talents and gaining as much experience as possible. Quite simply, the more you have the better choice of better paid jobs you will have.

It makes good sense to review your personal marketability from time to time, even when you are embarked in your career. Do this approximately once every 12 months. Look at ways in which you can improve your marketability. In this chapter we will look at practical ways in which you can do this.

All the main banks provide exactly the same service. They process cheques, issue cash, take deposits and provide overdrafts, loans and mortgages. There is very little difference in the service they provide. However, the banks try to differentiate themselves from their competitors by providing better customer service. The employees of each bank are instrumental in creating this difference.

Adding to your qualifications: choosing a course of study or training

Why undertake further study or training?

Many people consider that once they have left school or college, or embarked on their careers, they do not need to undertake further study or training. While this approach has not been a problem in the past it is becoming increasingly inadvisable. With galloping changes in technology and the way things are done it is very easy to fall behind. It is widely recognised by many personnel trainers that most people cannot hope to operate in a full-time job and keep abreast of all changes in, for example, technology that apply to it as well, without devoting time and effort to the process. This means that time should be allowed for further study and training and built into your schedule.

Further study or training is particularly relevant to work returners or job changers but really there are very few people that cannot benefit from it.

There are many advantages of further study or training. It can help you do your current job better, and save time. Most important of all it can also open doors to promotion, or qualify you to apply for a better job.

Could you benefit from further study or training?

If you answer yes to any of the following questions then a period of further study or training could be beneficial to you:

- Are finding it difficult to cope with new ideas or concepts in your current work?
- Are there areas of your work that you do not feel comfortable with, but never seem to have time to bring yourself up to date with them?
- Are you unable to apply for jobs you feel you could do well because you lack certain key qualifications?

■ Are there changes in laws or codes of practice pending or likely that will demand you are qualified to do the job you already do?

Points to consider when choosing training or study

Not any period of training or study will benefit your career. It is important to choose something that will be as relevant and useful as possible. These are the points you should consider when choosing your training or study:

■ Is it relevant to your current job, or a future job you wish to do?

■ Is it training or study? Training tends to be regarded as a practically-based instruction, whereas study tends to involve an academic element.

■ Is it essential or optional? If it is essential when will it become essential?

■ Is it provided by your employer or not? The advantage of employer-provided training is that it is likely to be highly relevant to your current job and undertaken in your employer's time. However, it may not be relevant to any future jobs you hope to do.

■ Will it lead to a nationally or internationally recognised qualification?

■ What will the qualification lead to, if anything?

When making your choice try to select a programme that satisfies as many of the criteria discussed above as possible.

Sources of help and advice

Often it is difficult to decide what to do about training and study without any outside help. Programmes of training and study change frequently in their availability, content and value to your future career. However, there are many sources of help and advice you can use. These are some of the sources you can try:

Your employer. It is normally in your employer's own interest to ensure that training and study opportunities are made available to you. However, not all employers do this, and not all have access to information on all of them, so do not rely solely on this source of help.

National employment service. Your local office can often tell you about opportunities, especially if you are or soon will be unemployed, or are returning to work.

Other government departments and offices. It is always worth contacting any other relevant government departments and offices as they often know about training opportunities even if is not their responsibility to promote them. Check with offices that deal with trade and industry. In many countries there are local agencies who deal with training and enterprise.

Charitable foundations. Many charitable organisations promote training opportunities, especially but not exclusively for disadvantaged or minority groups. If you know of any charities that help people in your particular situation then it is worth asking them for advice on training and study opportunities. For example, there are charities which help women from ethnic minorities and also charities which assist students to find suitable further training.

Schools, colleges and universities. Don't neglect the help and advice that is available from your school, college or university.

Your local library. Libraries are normally a good source of advice in this respect. Ask if there is a librarian who deals specially with information on training. Many libraries also have access to computerised databases.

Private training organisations. As well as training and study opportunities provided by employers, government departments and educational institutions a number of private training organisations now provide training courses. They offer courses and training in a wide variety of business and industrial subjects varying in length from several weeks down to a day, or even less. Although they do charge fees these may be covered by your employer, or grants may be available.

To find out about these opportunities look in your local newspapers, or 'Yellow Pages'.

Case study: A look at the UK leisure industry

Several leisure employers, mainly larger companies, provide their own training programmes leading to their own in-house qualifications. Alternatively, they may provide training programmes which allow you to obtain NVQs in Sport and Leisure, Catering and Hospitality or some other related area. With a large employer NVQs may be administered in-house. With a smaller employer these may be administered by a local college or training organisation, although the costs are normally covered by your employer.

The Institute of Leisure and Amenity Management (ILAM), The Institute of Sport and Recreation Management and other professional associations also have education and training programmes which lead to NVQs and/or their own professional qualifications.

Leisure industry employers also offer modern apprenticeships and national traineeships.

How to improve your experience

Why is experience important?

Although it used to be said that qualifications were a passport to a job it is now more often the case that qualifications plus experience are the passport to a job. And, since so many people have qualifications it is the experience that is the deciding factor. This is why experience is important: it shows the employer that you cannot only claim to be able to do the job but that you can actually do it.

Giving people experience by way of a training course or on-the-job training is expensive both in terms of delivering the training and in terms of the working time lost. This is the real value of experience: to many employers the fact you have experience is regarded as valuable training at someone else's expense!

In a competitive world it is best to have as much experience as possible and to develop your experience as widely as possible. You never know when it might come in useful for your current and future job. It is a good idea to regard experience as a truly valuable asset – look after it and develop it to its fullest potential.

Could you benefit from further experience?

If you answer yes to any of the following questions then a period of further study or training could be beneficial to you:

■ Are you asked to do things at work which you feel you are not equipped to do?

■ Are you asked to do things at work which you turn down because you know you would not know how to handle them?

■ Do you see jobs advertised which you would like to apply for, but experience is a bar?

■ Do you see others doing jobs which you feel sure you could do, but you lack the know-how that would enable you to do the job?

■ Have you been in your current job less than six months?

Ways of developing your experience

There are various ways of developing your experience. Some of these are formal, where you or your employer purposely set out to develop your experience. These are more likely to be available in large companies, where time is set aside for experience building activities. In smaller companies experience building activities may be organised informally. That is, you build up your experience as you do the job. These are equally valuable but you may have to take the initiative to develop them.

Here are some good ways in which you can develop your experience:

- *Volunteer for special projects that are not normally part of your duties*. These are normally stretching experiences, yet if they don't go well you can't be blamed since they aren't part of your job!

- *Offer to stand in for colleagues, preferably those doing jobs at a higher level than you, during holidays or other absences*. These provide you with hands-on experience with absolute responsibility and you also often receive practical support from your colleagues that other experience-gaining activities do not provide.

- *Shadow the work of your colleagues*. You can do this simply by showing an interest in what they do and asking them to explain their methods and ideas to you.

- *Take additional part-time jobs where these don't conflict with your current job*. For example, work in a pub or shop to gain customer contact experience.

- *Undertake voluntary work*. Contact your local clubs, societies, charities and other organisations and offer to help out in a way that will enhance your experience. For example, if you're an accountant looking to widen your experience, offer to handle the finances of a local charity or society. They'll normally welcome your offer and won't expect you to have any specialist experience or qualifications.

The importance of properly documenting your past experience

Gaining experience can be valuable indeed to helping you succeed in the jobs market. However, gaining the experience is not always enough in itself. You should try to prove it where possible. This can best be done by ensuring that all the experience you gain is documented.

Documenting your experience shows a well organised and methodical approach to your work. It is also increasingly becoming the case that employers expect to see some evidence of experience as some employees have tended to exaggerate or even falsify their experience in the past in order to secure the job they want.

It is a good idea to keep a file which documents your experience and add to it as you complete further experience-boosting activities. If you haven't documented your experience to date look back and see how you can collect together evidence of your experience to start your file.

Here are some ways in which experience can be documented:

■ Maintain full written details of each job you have done including employer, description of the duties involved, key responsibilities and your reason for leaving. Keep contact addresses where they are still current, preferably with the name of someone who can vouch for your experience.

■ Keep training manuals and operational handbooks that show what you did.

■ Keep any evidence of projects you worked on.

■ Keep any evidence of special achievements. For example, 'Employee of the Month' awards, or documentation that shows you achieved targets or, for example, that you were paid a bonus as a result.

■ Collect open testimonials from all previous employers. Ask for them when you leave whether they are required by a subsequent employer or not. Remember that if their writers move on (or the employer closes down) you may not be able to obtain them so easily.

■ Keep in contact with past colleagues who are willing to provide closed references. That is, references which you do not see. Because these references come directly from the referee they often carry much more weight with future employers.

■ Keep any relevant press cuttings if you or your company have ever been featured in the media.

■ Keep any letters of thanks and commendations you might have received from customers. If they have been sent to the company but apply to you then ask for copies at the time.

■ Keep any certificates, whether they are for formal qualifications or just internal training courses.

There are really no limits on what documentation and evidence you can and cannot keep. Anything that shows you have done what you say you have done is valuable. If necessary, provide either the originals or copies to prospective or future employees.

Remember confidentiality: remember that evidence of your experience may provide inside information about your employer's business to a prospective employer who may be a competitor. In these cases screen the evidence you provide in order to maintain confidentiality as a breach may place you in contravention of your contract of employment with your current employer.

How to benefit from work experience, placements or exchanges

What is work experience, a placement or exchange?

Work experience, placements or exchanges are all methods which allow you to sample a type of work for a short period. They are useful for several reasons. Firstly, they allow you to decide whether or not you would like to do that work. However, they are also important skills boosters. They offer an opportunity to learn new skills that you would not otherwise encounter and which you can use to improve your marketablity. The further advantage of these programmes is that they are normally provided and paid for by employers. Also, probably because of this, employers rate them very highly as experience boosting activities.

Work experience is a period spent finding out what it is like to do a particular job. This is normally a short period from a few days to a month maximum. It may involve observing or shadowing someone who already does the job rather than doing the job itself.

A placement is a longer period of doing a particular job which can last from at least a month to a year. It is particularly common when used in conjunction with educational courses and in certain professions, such as medicine. Someone undertaking a placement often does a particular job and frequently these are jobs reserved for placements. They are known as internships in some countries.

An exchange scheme is a type of work experience or placement where two people, normally undertaking a similar job, exchange places for a period. This may be simultaneously or at different times. It is designed to give a taster of how things are done in different organisations with the view of broadening the outlook and experience of the exchangees. Exchange schemes can be conducted within the same country although they are most usually between individuals doing a similar job in different countries.

Could you benefit from one of these programmes?

If you answer yes to any of the following questions then a period of work experience, a placement or an exchange scheme could be of benefit to you:

■ Are you still undergoing formal education, i.e. are you at school or college?

■ Have you been in your current job less than six months?

■ Are you at a cross-roads in your career, with choices to make?

■ Are you dissatisfied with your current job but do not know what the next step might be?

■ Are you hoping to go for promotion or apply for another job but lack the necessary experience?

■ Do you feel uncomfortable about handling certain aspects of your current job and need further help?

■ Have you a responsibility for development in your type of job, but lack ideas on how to develop?

Finding a scheme

Finding a work experience, placement or exchange scheme is not always easy. Many such programmes exist but they change frequently and it is difficult for any single point of information to know about all the schemes which apply to your situation. Here are some sources:

■ *Ask your employer.* It is in their interests for you to participate in such schemes and there are sometimes officially organised programmes. If one does not exist then ask if you can create one, perhaps by suggesting an exchange with a company in a similar business elsewhere, or a branch or subsidiary abroad.

■ *Ask your school or college.* They normally have contacts with employers. If not, or if these links are unsuitable for your needs, ask for their support in developing a new programme.

■ *Ask the national employment service.* They can be particularly helpful if you are unemployed, or a returner.

■ *Ask government departments.* Especially those involved with education, employment and industry.

■ *Ask professional organisations and societies.* These are probably one of the best sources of work experience, placements and exchanges and often have links with professional organisations abroad. If not, ask for their support in creating a new link. You do not normally need to be a member to enquire about programmes, although you may need to become one in order to participate.

■ *As a final choice, approach other companies*. Even if they do not have a scheme in operation they may be willing to create one for you. With all these schemes there are benefits to be had for all the parties involved, not just the employee.

Is the scheme suitable?

It is very important to make sure that your work experience, placement or exchange scheme is suitable. Often the prospect of taking part in such a programme is very tempting – especially if it involves a period abroad – but it is important to think about the opportunity in rational terms and ensure that it is not only beneficial but a good use of your time. Remember that such programmes can take up several weeks, months or even a year and therefore it is important that your time is at least as well spent as it would be if you had stayed in your job. The following checklist will help to identify the most suitable programmes:

■ How long does the programme last? Does this fit in with your other commitments?

■ How far does your employer approve? Are they keen for you to participate or are they merely willing for you to take part?

■ What costs are involved and how much is the cost justified? Will your employer pay or contribute? Remember, even if they pay there may be other expenses you will have to meet, such as living expenses.

■ Is a grant to fund or partly fund the cost available?

■ Does the programme involve observation or participation? Programmes which involve participation are more desirable as they literally give you 'hands on' experience.

■ Does the programme provide you with a formal qualification? These programmes are more desirable.

■ What skills and experience will the programme provide you with? For example, the chance to develop foreign language knowledge or computer know-how. The more skills and experience you can develop the better. Also, skills and experience that are documented are generally more valuable than those types of skills and experience which are difficult to prove.

Getting the most from your scheme

Work experience, placements and exchanges are informal ways of developing your skills and in many cases very loosely defined without clear targets or objectives. It is, therefore, important that you take responsibility for guiding the scheme yourself and obtaining the most benefit from it. While it is unlikely to undertake such a scheme and not gain great benefit from it there is much you can do to maximise the benefits from it, and hence maximise the benefits to your future career. For example:

■ Go into the scheme with an open mind. Things are unlikely to be done the way you are used to. Consider whether and how much better these are than the way you might do them. This is one of the benefits of such a scheme.

■ Ask questions if in doubt. A scheme is very much a learning experience, even though it is a formal educational course.

■ Look for opportunities to contribute to the work being done or the service being provided. This is particularly beneficial with a work experience scheme where you may be merely shadowing someone else's work. Obtain evidence that you have done this where possible.

■ In the case of exchanges decide whether you or your partner should take the lead in advance. Do the same, only in reverse, when they return to you.

■ Obtain any qualifications that may be offered to you during or after the programme.

■ Obtain evidence of what you have done, even if just a letter from an employer briefly explaining what was done.

■ Arrange a briefing when you return to normal working. Share the benefits with your colleagues and see how they could be implemented in your organisation. This will also help you to readjust to your 'normal' job, as your views and ways of working may have changed considerably following your experience.

Preparing a professional CV

A curriculum vitae, or CV, is a statement of your personal details, educational and work history to date that is presented in a standardised and concise format. It enables the employer to receive at-a-glance information about you in a quick and easy-to-absorb way. It is also known as a résumé or bio (biography) in some countries.

Nowadays a CV is becoming essential for all employees at all levels. If you do not have one you should certainly prepare one. Also, if you have one, keep it up to date as changes occur. In simple terms, your CV is your 'shop window' and a vital tool to help you win in the jobs market.

A good CV should:

■ Be concise. A CV isn't meant to be a life history. It is supposed to be a résumé, mainly of your educational and work history. The term résumé, used in many countries, is much more descriptive than the term CV.

■ Be clear. A CV should make communicating your personal information easier, not more difficult than, for example, writing a letter.

■ Contain all personal details. This includes your name, address and telephone number. A CV is often used as an address book by the recruitment people. Make sure it shows how to contact you at a glance.

■ Contain educational details. These should include schools and colleges attended, qualifications studied and grades obtained.

■ Contain work details. These should include all employers worked for and a brief address, job title and, if space permits, a few words on your experience and responsibilities.

■ Be presented in a certain way. There is a standardised style for CVs with slight variations permissible, but all CVs should follow the accepted way of doing things. Don't try and improve on it, even if you think you can.

Using a CV service

One alternative when preparing a CV is to use a professional CV service. These services take your personal information and assemble it into a professional CV and even provide you with printed copies to send out with job applications.

The advantages of CV services are that they usually know what makes a good CV. They also usually present your CV very professionally which is good if you do not have the appropriate equipment to type or wordprocess it yourself. Another advantage is that they will be more objective and may be able to spot points that you should include, as well as identify information that you have included that could be omitted.

The disadvantage of using a professional CV service, apart from the cost, is that it will very often be obvious to the employer that you have used a CV service. This may count against you in that they may consider you are unable to prepare a CV yourself.

If you do use a CV service here are some points to bear in mind:

■ Make sure the CV service has all the information they need to prepare the CV properly. Provide them with source material (e.g. exam certificates) rather than second-hand information, where possible.

■ Ask them for an appraisal of how well the information you have provided will work up into a CV. Especially ask for their advice on any gaps there may be in your experience or qualifications which need to be filled.

■ Recognise that different CVs may need to be used for different jobs. For example, highlighting the qualifications and experience that are most appropriate to the job for which you are applying.

■ Look for a service where you can get an unlimited amount of copies for a moderate additional fee and where changes and improvements can be made as necessary.

Exercises

1 Using the information already given in this chapter list the sources of further advice which you feel might be of use to you.

2 Find out where these sources of help and advice are available in your area. Make up an address book of contacts for use in the future.

Compiling your own CV

When writing your curriculum vitae remember that it is one of the most important documents in your job application. It provides all the relevant information about you on one simple sheet of paper. The employer doesn't have to go wading through a letter to extract what they really need to know. A well prepared CV is also evidence of the fact that you can work professionally and to a high standard, both of which are very important qualities for all types of work.

If you don't presently have a CV then it is a very good idea to compile one now. It will then be ready and waiting to send off with your applications. If you do have a CV then review it before every application to make sure it is as up to date as possible.

There is no reason why you cannot write your own CV and modify the concept slightly to suit your own requirements. However, there are some basic guidelines which will should be followed in all CVs:

■ Always head the page with CURRICULUM VITAE. This is a simple point which is often overlooked but it helps to draw the reader's eye straight to the document.

■ Always include your full name. Put your first name first, followed by any middle names and your surname.

■ Always give a full postal address, including post code. If you have more than one address (for example, you are a student at college during term and with your parents during vacations) then give all addresses so that you can always be contacted.

■ Always give a telephone number, with different day and evening numbers if possible. Often interviews are given to people who can be called in at short notice.

■ Put your educational history next. Younger applicants should include all schools attended. Older applicants may normally just refer to their further and higher education. State all qualifications obtained and if they are not widely known then write them out in full rather than just using abbreviations.

■ The next section should cover your work history. Start with your current job and work back to at least your last three or four jobs (if applicable).

■ It is a very good idea to state your main responsibilities in each job and also, if space allows, your main reason for leaving.

■ If there are any gaps in your educational or work history (for example, gap years or periods of unemployment) then include these and say what you were doing. This is much better than saying nothing which tends to create suspicion.

■ Mention any vocational qualifications you have separately from your academic qualifications since these are of more interest to many employers and so it is very important that these stand out.

- Always say a few words (but not too much) about hobbies and interests as, again, this will help you to stand out from the crowd.
- If you are applying for a job where languages are either necessary or would be an advantage then always include this in a separate section. Also state your level of competence, for example, beginner, intermediate, advanced. Be truthful here and do not be tempted to exaggerate.
- There is no need to sign a CV, but it is a good idea to date it. This shows that it is up to date and that you have taken the trouble to update it before sending it in.

The sample shown in Figure 2.1 is a good example of how to set out a CV, although it is perfectly acceptable to change the layout slightly to suit your requirements. In all cases your CV should be clear and professional looking.

Presenting your CV

Presenting your CV professionally is as important as writing it professionally. Some employers use the 'glance technique' as a way of selecting CVs for further consideration. CVs that are presented professionally are considered to identify the most suitable candidate. There is very little proof that this technique is effective but, nevertheless, it does operate, most usually as a screen to reduce the number of applicants selected for interview. As with writing a CV there are no official rules on presentation but the following will serve as good guidelines:

- Type on one side of one A4-sized sheet of paper only. Avoid using more than one sheet if at all possible.
- CVs should be typed or wordprocessed, never handwritten. Originals are best but photocopies are acceptable if the quality is good.
- Never fax a CV unless specifically requested. The quality of the fax will never compare favourably with those applicants who have sent an original CV.
- Use good quality, white, cream or light blue paper with black ink or print. Apart from for the purposes of clarity your CV may need to be photocopied and black print will reproduce best.
- Send your CV in an envelope which is large enough so that it doesn't need to be folded, if at all possible.
- You can present your information in date order or reverse date order as you prefer but you should use the same method for all information presented on the CV.

CURRICULUM VITAE

Janet Johnson

Home Address:
33 Any Avenue
Anytown
AY1 1AB

Tel.: 0000 000000 (Day) 0000 000000 (Eve)

Date of Birth: 1 January 19xx

Education:
1983–1988: City High School, Anytown. I followed a course of
study leading to O level qualifications in the following subjects:
Mathematics (grade C), English (grade C), Chemistry (grade C),
History (grade B).

1977–1983: The Village Primary School, Anysville.

Career:
1992–Present: Manageress, The Perfumery, Anytown Airport. I am
responsible for the management of the perfume and cosmetics
counters within the shop. This includes overall responsibility for
personnel, display, accounting and for meeting sales targets.

1989–1992: Sales Assistant, The Department Store, Anytown. My
position involved training in all aspects of the retail of perfumes and
cosmetics including display, demonstration and sales techniques.
Reason for leaving: to take a position involving more responsibility.

Other qualifications: Diploma in Sales Promotion & Selling.
Hobbies and interests: Swimming, listening to music.
Languages: I speak a little conversational French and Italian.

Figure 2.1   A sample curriculum vitae

Ways to improve your CV

Once you have prepared your draft CV it is a good idea to sit down and examine it closely and consider what small improvements you might be able to make which will improve the overall appearance and impact of the document. Here are some details which, although small, can help to improve your CV:

- Give telephone numbers where you can be contacted at all times. If applicants need to be called in at short notice it is often those who can be contacted immediately who will be selected.

- As well as your job title say something about your main responsibilities in that job. Job titles are very undescriptive and, at worst, misleading.

- Explain anything that is not immediately obvious or which may be misunderstood. Before using abbreviations consider whether they are likely to be understood by the reader.

- Go through and delete the obvious or anything that is duplicated. It is, for example, normally a waste of space to include a date of birth and your age.

- Older people should delete ancient history! This relates to anything that happened over 20 years ago, unless it is clearly relevant to the job for which you are applying today.

- Younger people should try to capitalise on every event, even part-time jobs and working holidays. It is much better to say a little about a lot of things, rather than try to pad your CV out if, for example, you have only had one job to date.

- Say something about personal interests, such as out-of-work interests, sports and hobbies. Be concise, however, as there is unlikely to be much room for this information.

- Attach a photograph to your CV. It helps it to stand out from the rest. A passport photograph should suffice unless there any instructions in the job advertisement or application form to the contrary.

- Have an unbiased third party read your CV for you. They are more likely to be able to spot mistakes, omissions and anything that does not make sense!

Developing social and business skills

Nowadays it is not only formal qualifications and formal experience that are important. Social and business skills can also be important. In fact, they can make the difference between getting a job or a promotion and not getting it at all. With many qualified and experienced applicants for jobs it can often be the case that extra qualities like these actually tip the balance and get you the job.

A business skill is a skill that can contribute directly to your work. For example, the ability to write a well structured letter or sell something successfully. A social skill is a skill that you use socially, such as being able to conduct or lead a discussion. Business skills and social skills are often intertwined. However, business skills are of most practical use to employers. Thus, always consider how your social skills can be redeveloped and used in the world of business.

Business and social skills that can be useful

Here are some examples of useful business and social skills:

■ *Getting on with people*. Very few jobs involve working totally alone. Employers like good people skills because they make for a happier and more productive workplace and better links with customers.

■ *Making a structured, well organised telephone call*. Anyone can make a telephone call, but not everyone can make one that achieves the objective of the call quickly and easily. This sort of skill is useful in jobs that involve contact by telephone, especially with customers.

■ *Giving a speech*. Your job may call for you to give a speech to customers or colleagues. The skill is also useful when giving presentations, training or generally giving information to others.

■ *Selling something*. A vital skill for salespeople to possess, but also a useful skill for everyone else, even if you can just sell your ideas convincingly to others.

■ *Organising things*. The ability to plan, organise, implement and run a particular event is always useful. The skills required to organise, for example, a party are partly the same as those needed to run a business event, such as a conference.

■ *Providing hospitality*. If you can entertain friends and relations at home then the same skills can also be useful in your work.

These are just examples. There are many other business and personal skills which can help make you more employable. The secret, if there is one, is to identify your personal skills and ensure that potential employers are aware of them by mentioning them in job applications and at interviews. These skills will attract employers.

How to develop business and social skills

If you feel that your business and social skills are insufficient for the demands of the jobs you are interested in then you should aim to develop them. The best way to develop business and social skills is by practising them in both business and social situations. The simple solution, therefore, is to take every opportunity to mix with people at work and socially. Try out your ideas and approaches and see which work best.

Here are some additional ways of building business and social skills:

■ *Voluntary work*. This is a very good way of developing contacts with more people at all levels. Often you will become involved with people in difficult circumstances, which is a very good way of developing and refining any skill.

■ *Clubs and societies*. Whatever your interest there is bound to be a club or society to suit you. It is also worth considering clubs and societies in other areas of interest since these will tend to stretch your skills to their fullest by encouraging you to operate in areas where you don't feel quite so comfortable. Clubs and societies which involve organising, giving speeches or team work (such as sports clubs) are especially useful.

■ *A part-time job*. This can be a good way of building new skills that perhaps aren't required in your current job in preparation for another job where they will be required.

Advice on dress and appearance

Dress and appearance is becoming increasingly important and will continue to be in the future. Firstly, it is interesting to look at why this might be the case. In most cases it is because a good standard of dress and appearance is one way of giving you a competitive edge. Today, many people are well qualified and trained. Not all are capable of presenting a professional appearance. In a straight choice between two otherwise similar people points like dress and appearance can help to swing a decision in your favour.

Another factor to consider is that service industries are growing in number and importance. These place more emphasis on appearance than do other types of industry.

Whatever type of job you are currently working in, or hope to get, it is always a good idea as part of your marketability package to consider your dress and appearance along the following lines:

■ Re-assess your dress and appearance from time to time. It's easy to get into a rut in this respect. Consider carefully: what impression do you give to customers? This is a very good way of deciding what impression you are likely to give to present and future employers.

■ Are there guidelines on dress and appearance which you should be following? Employers may give the impression that it 'doesn't matter', but this is rarely the case if guidelines are in place. Some companies have written guidelines or a dress code which is there for a reason even though many people ignore it.

■ Take a step back. Does your current dress and appearance really fit in with the image you wish to project or are required to adopt? What changes could you make to project the right image?

■ If a uniform exists don't try to modify it for your own purposes.

■ A good tip for interviews is to wear the same sort of thing (or as near as possible) as you would wear when working in the job itself.

A profile of the ideal employee of the future

It is difficult to judge exactly what makes up the ideal employee. However, here are a few pointers which might help you. While it's not always necessary to conform with the profile of the ideal employee it may give you a few pointers as to what type of qualities employers look for in their employees.

Good people skills. A very large number of jobs nowadays involve working with the public, so it is necessary to have good people skills. You must like working with people, talking to them, understanding their requirements, helping them and also, in some cases, helping to understand their problems.

Experience of working with others. Previous experience of working with others, especially with the public, is a boon in many types of work, especially those that involve direct people skills. If you have just left school or college, or are new to the industry, then a part-time or summer job which has involved you in working with the public would equip you very well for a full-time job or career and enhance your suitability in the eyes of employers.

Customer care skills. Many companies nowadays, especially in sunrise industries, are service organisations of some kind. For example, they do something for the customer rather than sell a product as such. So, looking after the customer satisfactorily is an integral part of the product you are selling, rather than subsidiary to it and it is best if you actually like meeting people's needs in this way.

Teamwork skills. Teamwork is important in most occupations but particularly so in service industries where members of staff come together to provide a service. In many jobs you will provide one part of the service while your colleagues provide other aspects of the service so you should be able to get on well with others. A restaurant is a good example of a business where many people, such as chefs, kitchen porters and waiters or waitresses work to produce the finished product, but teamwork applies to many other industries also.

Financial acumen. Financial skills are useful if you want to work in, mainly, the private sector and also sometimes the public sector. Most commercial companies nowadays work in a competitive environment to a tight budget and so it is important, especially for those in supervisory and management positions, to be able to budget, handle and account for money.

Language skills. Although it is by no means necessary to have language skills to succeed in the jobs market it would certainly help anyone's career. Most employers (and increasingly in the future) are interested in doing business with other countries if they do not actually do so already. Having a knowledge of one or more foreign languages would allow you to deal with customers and suppliers abroad. These skills are in short supply and you can often earn more if you have them. Having a knowledge of a foreign language would also mean you could work abroad at some stage if you so wish.

Summary

■ Marketability will become increasingly important in the future. It is the key to better jobs, better pay and better prospects.

■ To make yourself more marketable, enhance those qualities which are of value to employers.

■ Further training and study can help improve your marketability.

■ Experience is valuable to prospective employers.

■ A good CV helps to market those skills and qualities which you have acquired.

■ Additional qualities like business and social skills, a good standard of dress and appearance can be the icing on the cake which helps tip the balance in your favour.

3 | WINNING WITH ADVERTISED VACANCIES

This chapter will explain techniques you can use to find a job from amongst those jobs that are advertised. It will discuss how to systematically 'scan' the advertised jobs market to obtain access to the widest possible selection of opportunities, how to select vacancies to apply for which offer the best possible chance of success, and introduce a 'campaign strategy' for making an application for an advertised job. However, despite the chapter title, we will also be looking at unadvertised jobs at the end of the chapter.

Finding and using newspapers

Even though there is a very wide range of media in which to advertise job vacancies, newspapers are still a considerable source of vacancies. However, the situation on newspapers varies from company to company. Some companies advertise all their vacancies in newspapers as a matter of course. Some companies never advertise vacancies in the newspapers.

Here are some pros and cons of using newspapers.

Pros:

■ An easy way of accessing a large number of vacancies.
■ Provides you with information on what the job involves, pay and so on before you apply.
■ Makes it easy to 'shop around' for the best jobs.

Cons:

■ Many employers never use press advertising.
■ Press ads tend to attract a huge number of vacancies, sometimes thousands.
■ Press ads can sometimes be misleading, thus wasting your time applying for the wrong jobs.

■ Press ads are most often used for hard-to-fill jobs. Ask yourself why this vacancy is hard to fill?

It is very important to recognise that newspapers are not the only source of job vacancies. In fact, some estimates suggest that only 10 per cent of all job vacancies are promoted this way. The best advice therefore is always to use newspapers, but never to rely on them as the only source of vacancies.

Which newspapers to use

Local newspapers are good for local vacancies, part-time jobs and temporary vacancies. *Free newspapers* are also good for local vacancies, part-time jobs and temporary vacancies.

Regional newspapers are most suitable for jobs located in your largest regional centres, or with regional or national companies who have a major presence in your area. They occasionally have national vacancies. They are normally most effective for jobs in the professional and managerial sectors.

Evening newspapers tend to be suitable for local and regional vacancies. They are also strongest for unskilled, semi-skilled and skilled vacancies.

National newspapers are most suitable for managerial, professional and skilled vacancies. They mainly carry jobs in the capital and major regional centres.

One point to note with national newspapers is that they rarely if ever carry a broad spread of vacancies every day. In most newspapers a different day is devoted to different types of vacancies such as media, teaching, secretarial and so on. To make the best use of these publications find out which day or days of the week the type of job you are looking for is mainly advertised.

International newspapers – the national newspapers of other countries – can be used if you are interested in working abroad. They are often available at major newsagents or you can also take out a direct subscription to them with a subscriptions agency (see your 'Yellow Pages').

If using international newspapers to look for vacancies then note that in most cases only executive and professional vacancies can be found by this method.

In a number of industries and types of work there are *specialist newspapers* which bring you news and information on that particular type of work. These are an excellent source of vacancies for that particular industry and should always be consulted. The vacancies on offer, however, are often quite specialist and not suitable if you are not experienced in that type of work.

If you do not know what specialist newspapers are published in your trade or profession then ask at your local library.

There are also some specialist newspapers dealing with job vacancies only. Check with your library, careers service or employment service. These provide a broad spread of vacancies across all areas of work and all geographical areas. They are good for gaining a snapshot of job vacancies overall although cannot hope to cover every possible vacancy.

Points to bear in mind when using newspapers include:

■ They have a limited shelf life. You must apply immediately for any suitable vacancy. In the case of a daily newspaper, employers expect to get all the most serious applications the same or next day, so it will not help to put off sending your application.

■ They tend to attract a deluge of applications. Your application may be just one of several hundred, or even several thousand. It is important that your application is not only top quality but that it stands out in some way.

■ They are sometimes placed to comply with regulations or procedures. In other words an announcement does not necessarily mean that a job is available. The vacancy may already have been allocated to someone who works for the same employer.

■ Press ads are sometimes used to test the water and see what sort of interest there is in this position. That is, an actual vacancy may not exist.

Improving your success with advertised jobs

Contrary to what many people think the process of applying for an advertised job is not as simple as sending in your application and then trying your luck. There is a great deal that can be done to improve your chances of success. This is becoming more and more the case as employers are deluged with applications, many of them of a high standard, and employers find it increasingly necessary to look for the applicant who has taken extra effort. The following points will help you to do this:

Read the ad carefully. The actual vacancy may differ considerably from that which at first appears is being advertised. Try to read between the lines and see what the job actually involves rather than what the job title suggests. This way you will increase your success rate.

Find out more background information if you can. Call to confirm the details. Try to find out more about the employer. If you know someone who works or has worked there or who might know anything about the company then try and find out what you can through them.

Follow the instructions exactly as to how your application should be made. If it isn't clear then contact the employer to find out the preferred method of application, such as letter or telephone application.

Split the process down into a more manageable two-stage procedure. Devise an application whose main aim is to get an interview. When you've done that devote all your efforts to being selected at interview. Don't send an application whose objective is to get an interview and get you the job as well!

Look for clues in rejected applications. If the last application didn't succeed then it's more likely it won't succeed again. Try something else when you next apply for a vacancy. When you are successful in being offered one job examine your application to find out what might have helped you in the process. Make a note of what techniques you felt worked for use in the future.

Don't expect to get a reply from all applications you make in response to advertised vacancies. Many employers do not respond, either because they receive too many applications or just can't be bothered. It does not necessarily mean that your application was unsatisfactory. It may never have been read. Being rejected following an interview usually means that your application was good but your interview technique was poor, not that both were poor.

Finding and using trade and professional journals

Trade and professional journals are becoming an increasingly popular source of vacancies. This is because it is generally cheaper for employers to use them than newspapers, which charge higher advertisement rates because their subscriptions are much higher. Also, as many trade and professional journals circulate internationally it allows employers access to the global jobs market.

Trade and professional journals are not just restricted to what are traditionally considered to be professional jobs. They are now found in all fields and types of occupation.

Pros:

- They provide access to more unusual and specialist jobs which are rarely advertised elsewhere.
- Because they have smaller circulations they attract fewer applications. The employer is less likely to be deluged with applications and so yours stands a better chance of being read.
- As advertising space is cheaper, the ad is likely to be larger and so there will be more information about the job on which to base your application.
- They are more likely to feature jobs outside of your immediate locality, or your region. This makes them a good choice if you are willing to move. They are also good for jobs abroad.

Cons:

- They tend to contain advertisements for jobs which require more experience. This is a disadvantage if you lack a great deal of experience.
- They tend to contain advertisements for jobs which require higher levels of qualifications. This is a disadvantage if you know that your qualifications are incomplete, or could be improved upon.
- The standard of applications tends to be very high. You must do what you can to make your application both of a very high standard and stand out.

How to find suitable trade and professional journals

Trade and professional journals can be difficult to find out about. They rarely circulate in newsagents and not all libraries stock a comprehensive selection on their shelves. In some cases, these publications are only available by individual subscription. Here are some methods of tracking them down:

- Ask your employer, as they may subscribe to them. They may even be willing to give you copies, or arrange a subscription for you, since the news and editorial content will also be of use in your work.

- Ask colleagues, and those you know in a similar type of work.
- Ask at the library. Don't just look on the shelves. Ask to speak to the librarian who deals with trade and professional journals. They may be able to recommend titles. Don't just rely on a search as vacancies may not be listed in obvious places.
- Ask trade and professional organisations. They often have their own publications and may be able to send you a list of others.

Tips when applying for these jobs

When applying for vacancies that are advertised through trade and professional journals you should remember that they are often different in nature to those advertised in newspapers. Here are some points you will find especially useful:

- Remember that these vacancies are often highly specialist. The standard of applications is likely to be very high and fewer people will apply for them, so each application may be scrutinised in detail.
- These vacancies arc more likely to be handled on a personal basis, and by more senior personnel. It is often a good idea to make an initial enquiry by telephone. This will help you judge how to couch a written application.
- As these vacancies can be more difficult to fill employers are more willing to waive the job requirements, if the candidate is otherwise suitable. It may be worth applying if you do not meet the requirements exactly, but make an individual approach first to find out if this is likely to be productive.
- Individualise your application, to underline the importance which you attach to more specialist vacancies. For example, write an individual application letter and avoid photocopied CVs.

Exercises

1 Make a list of newspapers, magazines and other periodicals which you know contain advertisements for the type of job you are looking for.

2 Spend a couple of hours at your nearest main library. Do some research. Ask the librarian. Make a complete list of every possible publication which contains advertisements for the type of job you are seeking.

Using the Internet to find a job

How big is the Internet?

The Internet is one of the latest developments in the job-hunting market. It is potentially one of the biggest developments in job-hunting ever. At present though it is not entirely clear how the Internet will affect the job-hunting process. So, it is best to use it in addition to other methods, rather than in exclusion to all other methods.

Remember that the Internet is essentially an international communications system. In this case allowing computers to communicate quickly and cheaply with each other. It is not an advertising medium, and it is certainly not an employment agency. This means that the Internet is only as good as the use you make of it. It does not possess any magical powers which will help you find that ideal job that does not otherwise exist.

Currently the Internet is most useful when it comes to international job hunting and you can benefit from the speed and cheapness that it brings to international communications.

Using websites

The number of companies which publish websites, which are in effect electronic catalogues or databases accessible through the Internet and linked together in a network known as the world wide web (WWW for short), is growing by the day. There are already estimated to be several million websites in existence and several thousand more are being added by the day. They are published ('hosted' in computer speak) by commercial companies, governments, public authorities, educational and medical organisations and even private individuals.

Although most companies operate a website for advertising or PR purposes it can also be valuable to the job hunter. A website is an excellent site of comprehensive, up-to-date information on the company to which you are applying. Some but not all companies also publish vacancy information on their websites, allowing you to read and choose the most suitable vacancies. Many of these companies also accept online applications which can be e-mailed to them immediately in response to vacancies promoted on their website.

There are two ways to make use of websites. Firstly, if you know of a company which you would like to work for then always check out their website for information and vacancies. Secondly, search for potential employers, using a search tool or browser. This is a piece of software which literally searches the Internet looking for sites which meet the description you have provided. Enter key words such as 'airlines' or 'engineers' and your browser will supply a list of companies working in those areas, either in one country or worldwide. You can also enter a general term such as 'jobs' or 'employment' for a list of all vacancies being promoted on various websites on the Internet, although this may produce far too much information unless you also specify a particular area of work.

While using the Internet can be rather hit and miss, remember that since an application can be sent in minutes at very low cost there is very little to be lost by at least trying these techniques.

Useful pointers when using websites include:

- Be sure to surf them thoroughly. Try as many key words related to the type of job you are interested in. For example, to find jobs in banking ask your browser to search for all related areas such as 'banking', 'finance' and 'accountancy'. If you do not you may miss many suitable vacancies which are listed under closely associated areas.

- Websites are sometimes months out of date, especially where companies fail to maintain them as thoroughly as they might. Check the publication date before examining the site. It will be mentioned somewhere.

- Realise that some companies still do not have sites, or they can be difficult to find. So, do not expect necessarily to find vacancies for all your preferred companies. Also use the traditional methods such as newspapers and journals!

- The web operates internationally. You may receive information about overseas subsidiaries or branches that is not really relevant to your needs.

- Be selective. If anything you will find too much information rather than too little. Think quality rather than quantity. Careful use of your search tool or browser is necessary to make sure you get only the information you require. If you're new to the Internet practice carefully in other areas of interest (e.g. hobbies) before using websites to find a job.

Using Internet employment agencies

There are now a growing number of Internet employment agencies setting up business on the Internet itself. These agencies work by promoting their services on a web page. Interested parties – employers looking for employees – can search the web pages looking for people who possess the skills and qualifications they require. When they select suitable people details or a CV can be e-mailed to them in minutes.

There is no doubt that the Internet employment agency is very futuristic and has a great deal of potential. However, there are bound to be many limitations. Not all employers are familiar with this method and, in fact, most do not use this method. It will take some time to become an accepted method of recruiting. Also consider the cost element. Most of these agencies charge the employee (not normally the case with employment agencies) and you need to be sure that this is money well spent.

Here are some points to consider when using an Internet employment agency:

- Most Internet employment agencies are new and may have very little in the way of a track record. Ask what their success rate is.

- Ask what you get for your money. The best type of deal is one where you get unlimited listing until you find a job.

- Usage of these agencies by employers is variable. Employers in computer based areas may make use of them, but in other areas it may be rare.

- Write your entry yourself. Try to give as many reasons as possible why the employer should consider you.

- Check the site yourself to make sure that the search system (which other people will use to find your listing) works properly.

- After you've checked the site, consider how you could modify your entry to give it the edge over other similar candidates that are listed there.

You can find a selection of Internet employment agencies by searching for key words such as 'employment', 'jobs' or 'agencies'. It is impossible to give a complete list of websites as they are constantly changing and expanding.

The BBC website

The British Broadcasting Corporation (BBC) is an enthusiastic user of the Internet and hosts a massive website, accessible by Internet users around the world. Apart from information on BBC television and radio programmes the BBC also has a job vacancies area within its website. This area lists all employment opportunities with the BBC and provides details of the job requirements, skills and qualifications required and application procedure. There are also facilities so that Internet users can make an immediate online application for any of the jobs.

The BBC jobs website can be found at
http://www.bbc.co.uk/jobs/jobnow.htm.

Using bulletin boards

Although the Internet is becoming used more widely it is still something of a specialist community where users tend to think of themselves as privileged and where special bonds are more easily created between users. You may very well find that your Internet service provider operates bulletin boards or runs forums where users can come together to place ads, notices or exchange ideas. If so, these places could be a good location in which to advertise your availability for a job.

Many Internet service providers also provide subscribers with the facility to publish a small website (normally restricted in size to 5Mb) of their own. For example, CompuServe is one of several service providers that provides this facility at no additional cost to the monthly subscription. This facility can be used to publish your own website advertising your availability for work. Check with your Internet service provider (ISP) to see if they offer this service.

Here are some tips if you decide to use this method of accessing the jobs market:

■ Choose the right location. You needn't restrict yourself to employment sections, as there may be other special areas where you can advertise. For example, for a legal post place a message in a legal forum.

■ Don't assume your message will be read – unless you make it interesting and catchy. The headline or title needs to be particularly powerful.

■ Give details and a contact point for further information. Provide a telephone or fax number as well as an e-mail contact.

■ Consider confidentiality carefully. With an Internet bulletin board you never know who may read your message, nor any literature such as a CV that you may despatch to enquirers.

■ Remember that the Internet is still largely in its infancy and you cannot yet rely on this method of finding a job. Use the traditional methods also.

E-mailshotting

Because the Internet is such a quick and cheap method of communication it makes sense to consider the e-mail facility for the purpose of e-mailshotting. When you e-mailshot you send details of yourself to anyone and everyone you feel may be in a position to offer you a job (or help you in any other way). While this is often uneconomic and impractical to do by post, when you use the Internet it becomes both inexpensive and fast.

Here are some pointers when using e-mailshotting:

■ Prepare a letter of application or introduction in the normal way. Try to compose an interesting title or introduction which the recipient can see as soon as they see their e-mail. Include a CV if relevant.

■ Make use of the special features of e-mail to attach images or even sounds where appropriate. This is a highly innovative use of the facilities the Internet offers.

■ Prepare an e-mailing list carefully. This might include contacts, associates, people in the business, companies in the business. Use the membership enquiry service of your ISP to do this if necessary.

■ Try to send e-mailshots to a named person where possible. They have a much greater chance of being read. If you wish, send a copy of your letter to several to people in the same company in order to give it the greatest possible chance of being read.

■ Try to be quite selective. Don't send out too many e-mails, which may give you a bad reputation for spamming, the Internet term for junk mailing. (Some ISP's have spamming controls so you will not be able to e-mail people unless you have their correct and full e-mail address.)

■ Always provide a telephone and snail mail address for replies. Remember that not everyone is yet fully up to speed on the Internet. Some people may also wish to speak to you in person before deciding whether you may be suitable for the job in question.

■ If the application is particularly important to you don't rely on e-mailing entirely. Send a conventional application as well.

How to 'read' a job ad

Probably the best way to win with advertised vacancies is to read the job advertisement carefully and correctly. Employers often put a great deal of effort into writing job advertisements (many are written by specialist copywriters) and they are designed to do one of two things, namely:

1 Attract exactly the right sort of applicant.
2 Filter out unsuitable applicants.

If you can read the job advertisement properly you can save yourself a lot of wasted time in applying for unsuitable jobs, and also focus more attention on the jobs that are just right for you. Here are some key pointers you should consider:

■ Check the job title carefully, and what is involved as well. Jobs titles can be a clue to the level of responsibility involved, e.g. 'supervisor', 'manager' or 'director', but can sometimes be misleading. For example, some jobs carry the title director but do not involve a directorship of the company and are suitable for those of a lower level of skill and experience than the term might suggest.

■ Check the salary. This often reflects the calibre of the type of person the employer hopes to attract. If it is substantially higher than your current salary, or substantially lower, the job may not be suitable. Check into what is involved as this is not always the case, but it should certainly alert you to a possible problem.

■ Check the experience required very carefully indeed. The experience required is usually a minimum guide. Never assume that the employer will overlook a lack of experience as this is usually one of the first things they look for when considering your application.

■ Check for the word 'must'. For example, 'must be a graduate'. There are very few cases where 'must haves' will be overlooked and applications from those who do not have the appropriate requirement may not even be considered.

■ Look for job titles which are similar to the job you do now, but where the level of responsibility is higher. Applicants already holding a similar post often receive favourable consideration because it is often assumed, rightly or wrongly, that they must be able to do the job.

How to tailor your reply

Reply is the right word in this respect. When applying for an advertised vacancy you should always structure your application as a reply to the advertisement in question rather than being just an application. This shows that you have selected the job carefully and taken the time to make a proper application for it.

By and large, every application of this type needs to be handled separately. You can standardise replies to a certain extent – for example by enclosing a standardised CV – but only do this so far as is reasonably practical. The person who prepared the ad or who is sorting applications almost certainly has a profile in their mind of the ideal individual for the post they wish to fill. Thus, they are looking for an individual and not a person who merely blends into the background with a standardised approach to their application, no matter how competent.

Importantly, at this stage, remember, you have selected a vacancy for which, you feel, you are ideally suited. Don't spoil your chances at this comparatively early stage simply by communicating badly.

Bear the following points in mind when replying:

- Reply in the method stated in the advertisement. For example, in writing, by filling in a form, by telephoning or whatever. In this section we will look at making an application in writing and more tips on applying by other methods are given later.
- If an individual is mentioned in the ad reply to them personally in your letter. This looks more individual and also ensures that the application reaches the right place.
- Be sure to mention the job title and reference if there is one. The employer may be advertising several completely different jobs at the same time and it may not be obvious for which one you are applying. Indeed, the employer may not take the trouble to decide which one you are applying for. This mistake is made by a large number of applicants, so it is a very easy way to give your application a head start.
- Keep referring to the job title. This suggests that you have considered your application carefully and it also reminds the recruiter which vacancy they are trying to fill – important in a busy personnel department.
- Pick out the key requirements of the job. Say how you comply with them.

■ Pick out what experience is required for the job and say how you have this experience. You can simply say that you have the necessary experience. It is much better to give a positive example, however, of how something you have done in your last job(s) links to the experience required for the new one.

■ Pick out what you will be expected to do if this is stated in the ad. Say how you think you can achieve this.

■ If there are any direct questions, such as 'Is this you?' then be sure to answer them although this can be done indirectly.

■ At all times address the needs of the employer. Think in terms of the benefits to them of employing you.

■ Refer to the next stage of the application process. For example, if an interview date is suggested say that you will be happy to attend on that date. Even if you aren't say so, it can always be changed later on.

Ways to make your reply get noticed

The application procedure for a job commences the moment that you read the job advertisement, not when you fill in a form, or attend for an interview. If you think of it this way there is a great deal you can do to get your application noticed.

And it is extremely important to make your application get noticed, if not stand out from all the rest. As many vacancies nowadays attract several hundred (or even thousand) applications for just one vacancy it is vital that your application gets noticed. If not, it will not even progress to the next stage, no matter how suitable you may be for the job. The following are tips on how to get your reply noticed.

Reply immediately. Do not wait a week or two in the hope that your application will stand out better when the flow of replies tails off. Whenever it arrives it will almost certainly arrive with many others and at least an early reply shows enthusiasm.

Check the instructions in the advertisement exactly. This includes both obvious directions and directions hidden within the text of the ad. With complex ads it is a good idea to make a list of instructions that you must follow and check them off as you have completed each stage.

Send exactly what is asked for. If you must fill in a form don't apply by letter alone. If you are asked to send a CV always send one.

Check whether the application should be handwritten or typed/ wordprocessed. It's almost always better to send a typed application which is clearer but if you're asked for a handwritten letter always send one. Some employees feel that they can judge character from individual handwriting, or they may even employ a graphologist to advise.

Use an unusual paper – such as blue or cream rather than white. Never use deep shades, however. Use a large envelope – large enough to contain your application without being folded. This stands out much better then a DL or C5 size envelope.

Send your application by some form of registered mail. When received these items are almost always stacked on top of all the other mail and hence receive priority attention. This can be particularly effective when applying to small organisations, where recorded items may carry something of a novelty value.

Address your application to the person who will be processing them by name, not just position. If a name isn't given in the ad, telephone and try to find out who it is. Everyone responds to their name.

If the advertisement says that you can call for an informal chat then always do so. Even if there is very little further that you want to know think of some questions to ask. Those who have already spoken to the recruiter will always stand out more at the selection stage.

Winning with unadvertised jobs

What is an unadvertised job?

An unadvertised vacancy may seem to be a contradiction in terms but it is actually a significant source of vacancies and will become more important in future. Those who access unadvertised vacancies will substantially broaden their choice of jobs, and of desirable jobs, compared with those who do not use this method.

The best way to describe an unadvertised vacancy is that it is a vacancy that the employer doesn't know that he or she has. That is, they have a need for additional members of staff but, perhaps, do not realise that there is a gap that needs to be filled, or are unaware that there is someone out there who could contribute to their company. Many unadvertised vacancies arise simply because employers, mainly small employers, don't have time to recruit new staff. Yet, should someone with the appropriate skills and experience come to their notice they would be quite willing to employ them. By making yourself that person who 'comes to their notice' you could just have found the job that is ideal for you.

Here are some pros and cons of pursuing unadvertised jobs.

Pros:

■ It opens up new opportunities that didn't exist previously.

■ It gives you access to vacancies that other jobseekers don't know about.

■ There is little or no competition in the application process.

■ It is very cheap from the employer's point of view, and so is attractive to them.

Cons:

■ It requires extra research work in finding people and places who may be willing to employee you.

■ The success rate is modest, so it can be frustrating to receive many rejections along the way to your ideal job.

■ Time can be wasted when employers later decide that they do not have a vacancy.

■ You could end up being recruited into an unsuitable post, with responsibilities other than those which you expected. It is important to be selective to ensure that the potential post you apply for is right for you.

Targeting employers with unadvertised vacancies

Although you can write to any and every employer asking about the possibility of a job – and many jobseekers do – you will normally be much more successful if you target suitable employers. These types of employers are those most likely to have unadvertised vacancies:

■ Small employers. Often don't have time to devote to recruitment, which is frequently 'no one's job'.

■ Employers in sunrise industries. They are more open to this method as a way of filling hard-to-fill vacancies.

■ Employers in remote or fast growing areas. Again, they are often very receptive as vacancies may have proved hard to fill by advertising locally. This is also a good way of finding jobs abroad, mainly in the countries that are slightly less popular with expatriates.

■ Employers who are advertising similar jobs, or even different jobs.

This shows they are, at least, in recruiting mode.

■ Companies who have recently been awarded new contracts. They are very unlikely not to need some new personnel.

To use this method it is important to do your own research. No one can give you a list of unadvertised vacancies. Look in newspapers, trade journals and periodicals. Use networking: keep your ear to the ground. If all else fails use trade directories or the 'Yellow Pages' as a mailing list.

Applying for an unadvertised vacancy

The easiest way to apply for an unadvertised vacancy is by letter. This avoids embarrassment if the employer is not prepared to consider a speculative application of this nature. It also gives the employer a better opportunity to consider the approach which in most cases will arrive unexpectedly. A telephone or personal application received in such circumstances is more likely to be dismissed. So, follow these guidelines:

■ Send a short letter of introduction, introducing yourself and offering your services for any suitable vacancy.

■ Try and find out who is the right person to contact with your enquiry. Call and ask the receptionist or switchboard for the appropriate name. It is usually more appropriate to contact a departmental manager (or the managing director in the case of a smaller company) rather than the personnel department who may not yet know that a need exists.

■ Don't be too specific about your skills and experience and the type of work for which you are applying. There may be several possible posts for which you could be considered and this will leave your options open.

■ Attach a CV as normal with this type of application.

■ Don't apologise for making an unsolicited approach. If the employer isn't interested this serves no purpose. If the employer is interested it will only serve to make you look less confident and less enthusiastic and so hinder the rest of your application.

■ Invite the employer to contact you for further details or to discuss their requirements. This is a much better way of conducting negotiations once a need has been established.

■ Avoid making telephone calls which are more likely to be dismissed out of hand than written applications. If you do, make sure you speak to someone who is in a position to give you a job. Don't ask the receptionist or leave a message with someone else. If the right person isn't available call back later.

Some important points to remember about unadvertised vacancies include:

■ Don't expect them to be easy to find. After all, they're unadvertised! You must do some digging for yourself if you want to discover this rich seam of vacancies.

■ There are lots of unadvertised vacancies, although it might not seem that way. You need to be persistent and determined.

■ This route is particularly suitable for top level vacancies, and all cases where you have a unique or specialised skill to offer.

■ With unadvertised vacancies it's very important to sell yourself professionally. Do whatever you feel is necessary to convince the employer.

■ The best rewards are reaped in the long term. If people don't need you now they may need you in three, six or twelve months. Try potential employers again in the future if necessary.

Exercises

1 Make a list of as many companies as possible who you believe may have unadvertised vacancies of the type you are looking for.

2 Consider each organisation you have listed carefully. Establish which of these companies *rarely* or *never* advertise their vacancies in the press.

Case study: John finds his ideal job 'unadvertised'

John Harris was a well qualified sales representative working in the pharmaceutical industry. Although he had a good position he wanted to move to a smaller, more progressive employer where he might stand a chance at gaining a directorship in the future. None of the jobs he saw advertised in newspapers and trade journals appeared to offer better prospects than his current position.

Instead of reading the 'Situations Vacant' section of his monthly professional journal John instead scanned the 'News' section carefully. Every time he read of a new company starting up in the business he sent off a copy of his CV with a covering letter. Within six months he was offered a position with a progressive new company in the industry. After a further six months he was promoted to sales manager, and after a further 12 months promoted to the position of sales director. John feels sure that his success to date has largely been due to his foresight in applying for 'unadvertised' vacancies!

Summary

■ Newspapers are a substantial source of vacancies, but always strive to use them all. Don't restrict your choice to just your daily favourite.

■ Trade journals and periodicals can lead you to many jobs you wouldn't otherwise know about. Research carefully, as many of them are little-known.

■ The Internet will represent a growing source of jobs for the future.

■ Unadvertised vacancies are a substantial and growing source of vacancies.

■ When applying, remember that a different approach is often needed for vacancies approached from sources.

4 | **WINNING WITH EMPLOYMENT AGENCIES**

This chapter will explain how to find a job from amongst those jobs that are handled by employment agencies. It will discuss how to find agencies that handle particular types of job, how to approach them and how to deal with them. It will focus on the 'do's and don'ts' that must be observed when introducing a third party into the job-seeking process.

Understanding what agencies do

To obtain a job successfully through an employment agency it is very important to understand exactly what an employment agency does. Very few employment agencies, if any, work on behalf of the employee. Most of them work on behalf of the employer and are paid a considerable fee (often 20 per cent or more of the annual salary) to do just that. Here are some of the criteria that they follow when they carry out their service:

- To find the right person for the job.
- To do so as cheaply and efficiently as possible.
- To keep the employer as their client by continuing to do the above in future.

The most important point to note is that the agency always operates at the behest of the employer. Normally the cost or inconvenience to the employee does not enter the equation. Most agencies regard the employee as dispensable, no matter what impression they may give. Once you understand and appreciate this point it becomes much easier to obtain a job successfully using this route:

Remember the following points:

- No matter how pleasant the agency is their first loyalty is to the employer.
- They do not owe you any favours.
- You do not owe them any loyalty, nor will they usually expect it.

■ They will select the best person for the job regardless of all other factors.

■ The impression you make on them is important, but not as important as the impression you make on the employer who, at the end of the day, makes the final decision on recruitment and accepts overall responsibility for that decision.

Getting the best from a national employment service

A national employment service (The Employment Service's Job Centres in the UK) can be a useful source of help and advice for many types of jobs. A similar service exists in most developed countries. Although they have a reputation for offering large numbers of unskilled, part-time and temporary vacancies they can be a useful source of information.

The main point about using any nationally operated employment agency service is that the service operates for the benefit of the relevant national government whose aim, mainly, is to control unemployment. The purpose of the agency is principally to find jobs for employees or, as with a commercial agency, to find the right employee for the job. If you bear this in mind and work the system for your benefit it can still be a productive source of help and information.

Here are some pointers to guide you:

■ Always register with the national employment service. It is necessary in order to claim any benefits you may be entitled to.

■ In most cases it is not necessary to be unemployed to register with the employment agency. Indeed, employers tend to prefer employed jobseekers and, since they are usually offered few from this source, this is a very good way of getting your name on to the shortlist.

■ Ask for details of any special schemes that may be in operation at the moment. For example, work trials, work experience and so on. Given the importance of experience nowadays they are always to your advantage, even if they do not seem so at the time.

■ Scan the vacancies on offer regularly, but do not assume that these are the only vacancies that these employers have. If an employer is promoting vacancies with the national employment service it is quite likely that they are in recruitment mode and have other vacancies also. Contact them direct and ask.

■ Ask the staff if they know of any other vacancies, or other companies that are or may be recruiting. They have a close personal knowledge of the local jobs market and also a personal knowledge of their own area.

■ Visit offices in all other areas in which you are willing to work. Do not assume that you can find out about vacancies in other areas from your local office. This is supposedly possible in theory but does not always work in practice.

■ Do not allow the staff to apply on your behalf or make telephone enquiries. Take the address details and do this yourself. Your application will appear much more professional to the employer.

■ When making your application do not mention that you have obtained details from the agency. If the employer is biased against people who look for jobs this way it may count against you.

Getting the best from private employment agencies

There is a great deal you can do to get the best from your application when working with a private employment agency. Firstly, remember that although private employment agencies are hired to recruit for specific vacancies and often follow a procedure of taking instructions, advertising and filtering applications, you do not only have to apply to them in response to advertised vacancies. You can apply to them at any time. Private agencies are often glad to receive speculative applications: if they can fill a vacancy using an applicant who makes an approach to them they can save a lot of money by not having to advertise the vacancy, yet they can still claim the same fee from the employer!

Here are some points to bear in mind when approaching a private employment agency:

■ Get to know which agencies advertise your type of jobs and find out where they advertise. Checking their entries in the 'Yellow Pages' can provide you with useful background information.

■ Make a list of agencies and check for their vacancies on a regular basis, at least monthly.

■ Read the ad carefully and try to read between the lines. Consider what type of person the employer is looking for, not necessarily the type of person the agency is looking for. Use the techniques covered in Chapter 3.

■ Ignore those parts of advertisements which aim to glorify the job and the employer. For example, 'our client is a major player in the textile industry'. Announcements like this are normally placed to flatter the employer (the agency's client) rather than be of any use to the employee.

■ Pitch your application at the employer, not at the agency. While this might seem odd remember that, at the end of the day, the employer makes the final decision.

■ Remember that interviews held with the agency are normally just initial or screening interviews, not the ultimate job interview. They are often designed to enable a shortlist to be compiled. Make the objective of this interview being shortlisted rather than obtaining the job as such.

■ If you don't want the agency to refer your application to certain companies (e.g. your current or previous employers) say so. Agencies will always abide by these requests but won't know unless you tell them.

■ If applying for a job abroad note that private employment agencies are illegal in some countries. In other countries they may handle only temporary or contract work.

How to make your application

When making an application for a job through an agency it is important to realise that there are slight differences compared with applying for the job direct. The following pointers will be of use when presenting an application to an employer through an agency:

■ Follow the application instructions carefully. They are often more complicated for jobs promoted through agencies, and more stages may be involved in the application.

■ If possible, telephone the consultant at the agency for an informal discussion before making your application. They can often provide useful inside information and your enquiry won't jeopardise your application, whether or not these enquiries are invited. In the case of senior positions, or more specialised positions, ask for an informal meeting.

■ Try to obtain more information about the employer (the agency's client). This can help you tailor your application. Never make an educated guess, which could be wrong.

■ Don't be afraid to challenge the agency about their requirements, or take up points that are unclear with them. Normally this won't jeopardise your application.

■ To resolve the difficulty of pitching your application towards the employer but submitting it to the agency prepare two cover letters, one to the agency and one to the employer. The employer will almost certainly be shown this if your application progresses to the later stages.

■ If an agency handling the type of work you do doesn't have a suitable vacancy at the moment then send them your details anyway. Most will be more than willing to keep them on file in case a suitable vacancy arises in future. It's also worth re-contacting them from time to time (every three or six months), since they are unlikely to keep your details on file indefinitely.

How to make your application stand out

It is particularly important to ensure that an application submitted to an agency stands out. Firstly, agency vacancies receive responses in the same sort of high volumes as directly advertised vacancies. Secondly, agencies are even more selective about the applications they choose for further consideration. The following guidelines will help increase the chances that your application is selected:

■ Make it as clear as possible. Use good quality presentation and only say as much as you have to. No one likes to read pages and pages or irrelevant information.

■ Present it professionally. It is always a good idea to type or wordprocess applications of this type. Because the recruiters are so used to considering applications the standards they expect are so much higher.

■ Provide all the information that is asked for. If you don't your application may be rejected automatically.

■ Provide some supplementary information as well, something that few applicants think of providing.

■ Make it distinctive in some way, while keeping the professional element. One good way to do this is to include a passport photograph.

■ Don't try to fool the agency if you don't have the necessary skills and experience required for the vacancy.

■ Make it easy for them. Every agency likes to fill a position as quickly and easily as possible. They make the same fee no matter how much or how little work is involved and they'd probably prefer to do less!

Headhunting: what it is and how to benefit

Headhunting is a process whereby, rather than you applying to an employer for an advertised job, an employer makes an approach to offer you a job. Although traditionally operating at executive levels this procedure operates at more levels nowadays. In many industries, especially where there is a shortage of experienced and qualified staff, employers are more than willing to go out and headhunt the people they want.

In the modern day jobs market 'gentlemen's agreements' about not poaching staff, or for that matter extreme loyalty to one's own employer, are considered old-fashioned. Therefore, you should be aware of this procedure and use it to your own advantage. The only proviso is that you should never divulge details of your employer's business during this procedure. This would be considered a breach of contract. Here are some pointers:

■ Be aware that headhunting goes on at all levels – in your industry and in your type of job. Never discount the possibility.

■ Look for the tell-tale signs, such as other employees in your company leaving to take up jobs with your competitors.

■ Recognise that your company's competitors are most likely to headhunt you, and it's usually the case of big companies poaching from small companies. Your larger competitors are most likely to want you.

■ If you're interested in being headhunted get to know those likely to headhunt in the normal course of business, but be discreet. Make sure they know that you're ambitious, or looking for another challenge. It needn't jeopardise your current position.

■ Know how to recognise camouflage job offers. Calls from competitors asking if you know of anyone suitable for their vacancy are an obvious method. Job adverts so tightly worded that they seem almost tailor-made for you are another. Don't be afraid to put in an application.

Cautionary note: watch out for mischievous and false approaches made under the guise of headhunting, designed to find out your employer's secrets. Never accept an offer of a job or resign from your current position until you have received a copy of the proposed contract of employment, and never divulge details of your present employer's business.

Case study: Denise fills the job for the agency

Denise Leman applied for several jobs through an employment agency, but wasn't shortlisted for any of them. She realised that because so few suitable vacancies were advertised by this method it could take her several years to find the job that she really wanted. Instead she decided to take a proactive approach. She sent a copy of her CV and a covering letter to every employment agency listed in the 'Yellow Pages'. Several months later after securing a job through one of these agencies she was surprised to find out that this agency had many such suitable vacancies available but, in fact, never advertised any of them, instead preferring to await speculative applications from jobseekers!

Summary

■ Before applying for a job through an agency try to appreciate how they work.

■ Recognise the difference between jobs handled by the national employment agency and private agencies.

■ When applying through an agency recognise the differences involved compared with applying direct to an employer. Try to use these differences to your advantage wherever possible.

■ Be aware of headhunting and how it operates. Take steps to bring yourself to the attention of headhunters if you are interested in being offered a job through this method!

5 | WINNING WITH NETWORKING

What is networking?

Networking is a method by which you can find a job by building up and using a network of personal contacts. In simple terms, it is a method you can use to find the job you want by using the 'grapevine', or by 'being in the right place at the right time'. The aim of networking is to publicise your availability on the jobs market, usually in an unofficial way, so that as many potential employers as possible will hear about you and consider you for any job vacancies they might have.

Networking is ideal for use by both those who are currently in work, as well as those not currently working, and can be used alongside the more direct methods such as applying for advertised jobs or using employment agencies. If properly organised it can give you access to job offers that just aren't available from other sources. Plus, it can place you in the very desirable position where employers want you to work for them, rather than the other way round as is usually the case.

Networking has operated for many years at the highest levels of society, especially amongst politicians who use networking to find important Government posts, or industrialists who use networking to find senior executive posts or directorships. However, today, this method of winning in the jobs market is used at all levels and in some types of work it is believed that over two-thirds of all jobs are found by the use of networking. You may even be networking to a certain degree already, perhaps without even realising it. If so, you will gain even greater benefits by organising your efforts into a proper networking campaign.

If you doubt the value of networking consider this: who do you first think of when you need, for example, a plumber, an electrician, an accountant or a solicitor? The answer is, almost always, someone who you already know or who is recommended to you by a friend – by far preferable to looking up a total stranger in the 'Yellow Pages' or a newspaper. The same applies when employers are looking to fill vacancies and the fact is that they frequently use networking in preference to other methods, certainly where more specialist and better paid positions are concerned.

A simple example of networking:

Telling your existing business contacts, or friends and relatives, that you are looking for a more interesting or better paid job in the expectation that they will share this 'news' with their contacts, friends and colleagues who may be employers looking to fill a vacancy.

A more advanced example of networking:

Offering your services to your local television station as someone willing to be interviewed about a subject on which you are knowledgeable with the aim of getting your name known as an authority on the subject and the person to hire.

How to plan a networking campaign

For best results your networking efforts should be organised as a proper networking campaign and not left to develop in a haphazard way. Here are some points you should consider:

Decide what your goals are going to be before you actually start. This will allow you to target your efforts more accurately, leading to the type of job offer you really want. It will also enable you to minimise any networking activities which could lead to job offers you do not actually want. For example, if you are currently employed your networking goal might be to get more responsibility, or a better paid job. If you are unemployed your initial aim might be to get ANY job.

Questions to ask yourself when deciding your goals include:

■ Do I want to stay with my current employer, i.e. get promoted?

■ Do I want more status or responsibility, in preference to more money?

■ Do I want more money, regardless of other circumstances?

■ Do I want to move to another company?

■ Do I want to work in a totally different type of industry?

■ Is there a particular company or person I would like to work for?

Thinking about where you want to be in one or two years' time will help you decide which networking techniques are most suitable for you to use.

Recognise and deal with any 'negative forces' that may be operating. Are there any drawbacks that may put a potential employer off once they find out about you through networking? For example, if you have been made redundant or even resigned from your last job this may count against you. Have positive arguments ready to counteract these negative forces. For example, have a good reason for leaving your last job (such as wanting to devote yourself to looking for a new job full time) and incorporate this into your networking.

Think about the practicalities. Be prepared to deal with responses. Assuming that your networking works, potential employers will need to contact you – and quickly. Make sure you are contactable: use a mobile telephone or an answering service so that you can be reached at all times. Have personal calling cards printed which you can hand out so that potential employers always know where to write to or telephone you. (This also shows you are organised and professional, both qualities which appeal to employers.)

Know what to expect and decide how to deal with it. Think about what you are expecting your networking to lead to and decide how to handle it effectively. For example, if you hear a 'rumour' that a job might be available will you write to the prospective employer, telephone them, or visit them in person? If you receive a definite job offer from someone who has heard you are available decide how you will respond. Will you accept it straight away or hold out for a better deal?

Have a 'Plan B'. Networking is to some extent an unpredictable business so you should have a contingency plan in case the networking methods you use produce fewer (or even more) leads than you expected. Although you might decide to start networking using only one of the main techniques, which we will discuss later, also have two or three techniques in hand as a reserve to use if necessary – and have them ready to roll at short notice.

Consider the confidentiality aspect. One of the advantages of networking is that it does not involve you in directly applying for jobs, thus making it ideal if you do not wish to jeopardise your standing with your current employer. If, however, you do not want your current employer to know that you are looking to move on you must choose only the most discreet networking techniques.

How to implement a networking campaign

Once you have planned your networking campaign you can proceed to implementing it. This is a good procedure to follow:

Decide on a launch day, when you intend to launch your first networking activity, and stick to it. If you are also applying for jobs through newspaper advertisements or employment agencies do not let any success or failure in those areas cause you to delay your plans. Networking works best of all in the medium and long term so short-term changes in your employment status (like a recent interview offer) should not be allowed to disrupt your campaign.

Make a 'splash' to start with. It will get your campaign off to a flying start and also boost your confidence if you make a big impact to start things off. For example, you might start out with a concerted letter writing campaign, or you might aim to call every radio or television station in your area with the aim of securing an interview.

Do something regularly. Make a determined effort to do something that will keep your networking efforts moving on a regular basis. For example, you might resolve to start one new networking activity each month, or even each week.

Work out a timetable. Plan things out as much as possible. This works especially well when you resolve to do something regularly, as discussed above. Remember that summer holiday periods and Christmas/New Year tend to slow the wheels of business down. So, you might decide to hold back on networking during those periods but plan a major event to 'kick start' the process at the end of the slow period.

Keep a diary of what you have done and what has happened as a result. It is a good idea to write down, daily or weekly, exactly what you have done (or not done) to contribute towards your networking campaign and what has happened as a result (e.g. expressions of interest or actual job offers). Even if 'nothing' has happened it is important to keep track of the fact that nothing has happened.

Review your progress regularly. Look back over what has happened on a regular basis, perhaps monthly. This will allow you to spot which methods have succeeded and which have failed thus allowing you to stop unsuccessful activities and repeat the more successful ones.

Practical ways to make networking effective

Here are ideas for some practical techniques which can make networking work for you:

Using personal publicity

Always make sure other people know who you are and what you do. The first rule of successful networking is often overlooked but it is essential that as many people as possible know who you are and what you do. You should go out of your way to make this clear to anyone and everyone with whom you come into contact.

This process need not be difficult or embarrassing. Whenever you meet a new person always be sure to mention your name and what you do. (It's as simple as saying something like 'Hi, I'm Emma White ... I'm in the insurance business by the way'.) Business cards are a very valuable networker's tool. So, whether you're in business or not have some printed with your name, address, telephone and occupation and hand them out when you meet a new contact.

You can start benefiting from personal publicity at a very simple level indeed. You can operate it with all your existing colleagues and acquaintances, neighbours, in shops you use, your doctor, bank manager, local garage, pub, tradesmen – even with parents of your children's friends when you meet them at the school gate.

Think of it this way: if you mention your name and occupation to ten new acquaintances, and they happen to mention you to ten of their acquaintances, and they happen to mention you to ten of their acquaintances then, very shortly, several hundred new people will know who you are and what you do and some of them are bound to be of use in furthering your career.

Using letters of introduction

Write letters of introduction to successful people. If you know of someone who you think may be able to help you with your career, or even offer you a job, then write and introduce yourself. Offer your services, or ask their advice. While it is true that not everyone will respond, people who have achieved success have often done so through great initiative and admire those who show similar initiative. A referral from a successful person can carry a great deal of weight.

There have been numerous press reports of job-hunters who have written to successful people such as Richard Branson and Sir John Harvey Jones and who have secured job offers and referrals as a result. However, you can use this method at a more local level too by mailing local business leaders, company bosses and so on.

Attend as many meetings as possible

If you are ever offered the chance to attend a meeting, seminar or training course then do not hesitate to go. The people you meet will all be in a similar line of work and, by the law of averages, many of them are bound to be in more senior positions than you and very possibly in a position to offer you a job. If such opportunities do not arise then make them: pay to go on relevant training courses, seminars, workshops, literary luncheons and so on.

Offer to give speeches and talks

Societies and groups are always in need of guest speakers. So, no matter how trivial you think your job, hobby or special interest there is a willing audience out there somewhere. You can get a list of all your local clubs and societies from your library. Once you have this write to the Secretary of all relevant clubs and offer yourself as a guest speaker.

It does not matter what type of club or society it is: there are bound to be at least a handful of members who are in influential positions and who are in a position to help you with your career.

Join clubs and societies

Golf clubs have a deserved reputation as places where deals are done with the actual sport itself very much taking second place. However, nowadays, this principle applies to almost every other club too. The clubs you join do not have to be professional or business based. In fact it is better if they reflect your own personal interests as closely as possible. You will find that there are people in authority, or who run or manage businesses at every club you might care to join including sports clubs, amateur dramatics groups, even the local stamp collecting or photographic clubs.

Donate your services

You should always look at the possibilities for donating your services. Donating them to charity is a particularly good idea. Whether you are a builder or a banker, a student or a housewife, there is sure to be a charity that could make use of your services on an unpaid basis. Apart from the satisfaction of helping a worthy cause you are sure to find that your name becomes known far and wide as a result. If potential employers can actually see the benefits you have brought to the charity they will very readily be able to see the benefits you could bring to their business.

Writing letters to the editor

You should try to write as many letters as possible to the editors of local, regional and national newspapers and any magazines which are relevant to your line of work. Be sure to mention why you are qualified or experienced to comment on the subject you are writing about in your letter. Since newspapers often print the names and addresses of contributors you may well receive many valuable offers this way.

Become a radio and television pundit

If you have a particularly detailed knowledge of a given subject then you should write to the producers of all relevant radio and television programmes and tell them about yourself. Programme producers are always looking for competent guest speakers – from lawyers to farmers and mining engineers to motor mechanics – to give a professional opinion on subjects as they break in the news or to use in other programmes. A single 2–3 minute television appearance, for example, is worth a great deal as a 'free advert' for your services.

The added advantage of this is that, given the power of the broadcast media, a television or radio appearance lends you immediate credibility with potential employers.

How to turn a networked lead into a job offer

The ultimate aim of networking is that it will produce either definite or possible offers of employment from employers who have heard about you from your networking publicity. However, in some cases, your networking will instead produce leads which require further development if they are to turn into job offers. Here are some pointers on how to develop a networked lead:

Always follow up a lead. If a potential employer contacts you as a result of networking always follow the lead up. Give them a call and volunteer more information about yourself, or offer to go and see them for a chat or an interview. You should do this even if they are not your ideal employer, or offering your ideal job, since you never know who else they might know and what further job offers it might lead to.

Know how to recognise a 'come on'. Often it is necessary to read between the lines when being approached by a potential employer, since some employers do not wish to be known for openly headhunting or poaching new employees. Signals that an employer may be interested in offering you a job but is afraid to ask outright include being asked for your help or advice on a particular problem, or being offered a part-time or temporary job.

Make it clear you are available. Do not assume that, even though you have networked, the employer knows that you would like to work for him or her. If possible, contact them by telephone or in person and state clearly that you are. Use a positive approaches by, for example, saying that you are looking for a new challenge, more responsibility, better prospects or a better salary package.

Send your CV. If you think someone may be on the verge of offering you a position but you are not entirely sure then send them a copy of your up to date curriculum vitae simply marked 'for your interest' or 'for your consideration'. This makes it clear you are interested in a job but does not commit you, nor the employer, to a formal application.

Write a letter of application. If all else fails write a formal letter of application for the job, even if it has not been officially advertised. This should make it crystal clear that you welcome the employer's positive response to your networking and are definitely looking for a job with them!

Exercises

1 Using the information given in this chapter make a list of those networking techniques which you feel are most appropriate to you.

2 Plan your own personal networking campaign.

Case study: How networking worked

Victor Obosa worked for a major bank, but after five years in the same position had become frustrated by the lack of opportunities for promotion. Victor registered with several employment agencies and scanned the newspaper advertisement columns every day, applying for numerous vacancies. He was offered two jobs as a result of these activities but neither of them matched his existing level of responsibilities nor exceeded his current salary. Victor offered his services as a Financial Manager, on a voluntary basis, to a local charity, working in the evenings and weekends. Two months later he was offered a management job with one of the charity's commercial sponsors (a major motor distributorship) at 30 per cent more than his current salary.

Summary

- Before embarking on a networking campaign, try to understand how networking operates.
- Plan a networking campaign carefully, deciding goals in advance, considering practicalities and so on.
- Once you have planned your networking campaign then proceed to implement it, deciding on a launch day, working out a timetable and regularly reviewing progress.
- Practical ways to make networking effective include using personal publicity, using letters of introduction, giving talks, attending meetings, joining clubs and societies, and so on.
- Learn to recognise a networked lead when it arises and follow it up.

6 WINNING JOB APPLICATION TECHNIQUES

This chapter will focus on how to prepare a winning job application, examining every aspect of the application process from finding out about a vacancy, right up to attending the interview.

How to interpret what the employer wants

When first applying for any new job it is always a good idea to think carefully about exactly what the employer is looking for before taking your application any further. This has two benefits: firstly, it will help you decide if the job is really for you and, secondly, it will help you decide how to put over your own personal skills and qualities to best effect.

The easiest way to decide what kind of person the employer wants is to read carefully the job advertisement, the application forms and any other literature you have been sent. This literature contains many clues as to the profile of the employee being sought, for example:

■ If the literature says that you *must* possess certain qualities then, generally, your application will not even be considered if you do not have them.

■ If the literature says that certain qualities are *preferred* then it is reasonable to assume that the employer will be looking for evidence that you possess these qualities in your application. If you do not possess them then you must be able to make out a very good case why other qualities you possess compensate for this.

Next, look at the type of business and the industry in which the employer operates. Look at the service they provide or the product they produce, and the types of people they count as their customers, and their existing employees. Take some time to analyse carefully what type of people you are likely to be working with and how well (or how badly) you fit the profile. It tends to be the case that, to borrow an old saying, 'birds of a feather flock together'! If you're not that sort of person then it is going to be more difficult to get that post. If, on the other hand you are, you automatically have a head start.

It is a good idea to call the company concerned, if there is time, and ask for any promotional catalogues or brochures which they may have. This can help answer the question above.

Analysing what the employer expects

It is a good idea to spend a few moments analysing the likely requirements of a potential employer before putting your application together. A good way to do this is to complete the chart contained in Figure 6.1 for each type of job you are interested in. The examples show how you might do this.

Work through this system for the type of job you are applying for and you will almost certainly learn a great deal about what the employer is looking for in your application.

Type of industry:	What they do:	What they need:
Banking and finance	Manage money	People who can work quickly and accurately. Probably computer literate.
Retail industry	Sell to customers via retail shops	People with good organisational skills. Good at dealing with customers.

Figure 6.1 Analysing what the employer expects

Only once you have aimed to understand the requirements of the employer should you progress to preparing and completing your application. By making yourself aware of their requirements in the first place you will be in a *much* better position to prepare a successful application.

How to tackle application forms

What is the application form designed to do?

It is important to realise that the application form is not just a method of recording and storing information. It is part of the application and employment process.

Many employers use the form as a screening exercise. Forms that are wrongly filled in are discarded even if the employee is ideal for the job. This may seem ridiculous and indeed it is, but this is the way things are often done.

Most employers make the application form part of the personnel records if you are subsequently employed. Future decisions may be made on it. If you are promoted you may be promoted on the basis of information supplied. If you have lied you may find yourself promoted into work which you are not qualified for. If you are found to have lied you may even be dismissed.

While bearing these points in mind let us look at the immediate uses of the application form:

- To make applications easy to handle.
- To record information concisely.
- To spot suitable applicants easily.
- To spot unsuitable applicants easily.
- To allow a direct comparison to be made between applicants.
- To provide a basis on which to ask interview questions.

Types of application form

Before completing an application form it is useful to look at exactly what it requires you to do. The following are some examples:

Simple personal information form. This type of form simply asks you to write in your personal details, such as name, address, previous employment history and so on. It is used to record basic information and make decisions on whom to interview.

Suitability questionnaire. This type of form asks leading questions, often requiring you to select an answer from a multiple choice on offer. It is often used as an easy way of screening out unsuitable applicants, for example, choosing certain options will mean you are not selected for interview.

Essay application form. This type of form requires you to give written answers to specific questions, such as, 'Why do you want this job?'. Your answers are often used as a tie-breaker to choose between applicants who are suitable in all other respects.

Application form with psychometric tests. This type of form is rarer. It will include psychometric tests such as puzzles or word games. It is a more sophisticated form of the suitability questionnaire and, again, is often used as a screen.

Many forms combine all these functions.

Do's and don'ts when completing the form

■ Do read the form thoroughly before you start.

■ Do take a copy and complete that before completing the original and submitting it.

■ Do follow the instructions exactly. This is sometimes used as a screen and those who don't obey the instructions are disqualified.

■ Do ask for help if you are not sure what any questions mean.

■ Do make a copy of the form before sending it off.

■ Don't send a letter or printout instead of a form, no matter how time consuming the form is to complete by hand.

■ Don't send a form with any mistakes or alterations. This could result in your form being disqualified. If you do make a mistake call and ask for a new form to be sent to you.

■ Don't leave any questions blank. If you don't have an answer to a particular question or the question doesn't apply to you then say so.

■ Don't give misleading or dishonest information. The form may comprise part of your employment records.

How to handle the information pages

The information pages are those pages on which you provide information and personal details about yourself. Many applicants are apt to see these as easy and rush through them without thinking. This is a mistake because this section is often used as a screen to filter out unsuitable applicants. Giving the wrong information may also be embarrassing later. Don't rush, take your time. If this section is completed perfectly then your application at least stands a chance of being considered even if the later parts of it (the parts not used as a screen) are not the best.

- Read these pages at least twice.
- Put your name as you normally use it.
- Don't make silly mistakes, such as putting the current year as your birth year or first and surnames in the wrong spaces.
- If you can't answer something for some reason, such as it isn't appropriate for you, say so rather than leaving a blank.
- If you have to answer in a way that doesn't fit the standard pattern explain why.

How to answer likely questions

The best way to answer suitability questions and psychometric test questions is honestly. If you don't then, at the very least, you could end up being offered a job which is totally unsuitable for you. At worst, you could be identified as a cheat by a psychometric test. These tests are often designed so that the answer you think is the best one is actually the very last option you should choose!

Essay questions, on the other hand, require more careful consideration. An essay question can be defined as a question to which the answer is more than a few words. It may be anything from a paragraph to a whole page.

The purpose of an essay question is two-fold. It is designed to extract information. So much is obvious. It is also designed to test how you can process and set out information. It may also give an indication of neatness of your written work as well.

These questions may seem tiresome, but they are normally easier than you think and a good way of impressing the interviewer. They are a very good way of identifying yourself as an outstanding applicant, even if your answers to the other questions in the application are merely mediocre.

Here are some tips on how to handle essay questions:

- Read the question carefully. The question may actually be very different from that which you expect.
- Read other essay questions, to ensure that your answer does not answer the other questions inadvertently, thus leaving you with nothing more to say in another answer.
- Decide your answer. It is normally best to put what you want to say rather than what you think you should say.
- Make a list of points to cover. Each point should equate to one paragraph in your essay.

- Cut out anything superfluous. Don't drag on into covering points that have nothing to do with the question. Keep your answer concise.
- Make sure you have answered the question fully. Be objective.
- Never give a 'yes' or a 'no' answer. Answers should be properly phrased in a sentence or phrase.
- If a given space is allocated to the answer don't feel that you have to fill it if you can answer the question perfectly satisfactorily in much less space. This is actually a good sign. However, try to avoid giving an answer that is longer than the space that is available. If you really have to you can attach a separate sheet – but try to avoid this if at all possible.

Here are some likely essay questions and tips on how to handle them.

They can be direct like this:

Why do you want this job? It is acceptable to mention personal benefits which you think you will obtain from the post but try to focus on employer-orientated benefits.

What can you bring to this position? Concentrate on your skills and qualifications and, particularly, past experience that you feel would be useful to the employer.

What would you do if...? It is always difficult to answer hypothetical questions, such as 'What would you do if a customer complained to you?' The best way to answer is to be honest, showing how you would deal with the problem in the most professional way.

Questions can also be indirect like this:

- You may use this space to give further information in support of your application.
- If there are any other points you would like to make in support of your application you may do so below.

Never leave this blank. It is one of the first sections the employer will look at. In this case, try to use all the space. The space allowed tends to suggest that this is the length of answer expected.

Try to add something to your application. Don't merely recap points you have already made unless you think they really do need to be recapped.

More do's and don'ts

- Do say that you want to further your career.
- Do say that you think you would enjoy the challenge.

■ Do refer to your experience, if any.

■ Do say that you realise the drawbacks of the job, such as working unsocial hours (if your job will require that).

■ Don't say that you would find the work fun.

■ Don't say that you think you would find the work exciting.

■ Don't say you are bored with your present job. (The reader will tend to assume you will also get bored with this job.)

How to improve your application form

The following are ways to improve your application form:

■ Proof read your application twice, once for the accuracy of the information and once for the accuracy of the spelling, grammar and so on.

■ Attach a photograph. You must do this if the instructions say so. However, you can choose to do this even if there is no requirement to send a photograph. It will certainly help to make your application stand out.

■ Have it read by an impartial third party. They may be able to suggest improvements, as well as spot any errors you have made.

■ Always send a covering letter with your application.

■ Follow seemingly strange instructions exactly. Read the instructions on the form carefully and follow them exactly. If it says write in block capitals, or in black ink, then do so. (This is often so that the form can be photocopied and distributed to several people. If you write in blue ink, for example, it may not photocopy well.)

■ Even if you have given some of the information in a covering letter or CV repeat it on the form if asked for. Do not put 'refer to my CV' as the person reading the application form may not bother.

■ Give full and complete answers. If you really need to say more than there is space for on the form then attach another sheet and refer to it on the application form. Only do this if you have to and keep the attached sheets to a minimum, but it is better than giving an incomplete answer.

Figure 6.2 illustrates a sample application form for you to study. You might like to practise answering the questions. Once you have the answers on paper you can then use them in just about any application form you need to complete in the future!

ANYTOWN ENTERPRISES PLC

Application for Employment

- Please complete every section of this form using a black ballpoint pen. If there is insufficient space to give a complete answer then please attach a separate sheet.

Position applied for:

Surname:
Forenames:
Marital status:
Single/Engaged/Married/Divorced/Separated/Widowed
Date of Birth:
Age:
Place of Birth:
Nationality:
Address:
Telephone (include area code):
Address of parents or
guardian (if different):

Please give any dates in the near future when you will not be available for interview:

Where did you hear of this vacancy?:

UNIFORM DETAILS

Female:	UK size:
Bust:	Waist:
Hips:	Height:

Male:	Chest:
Waist:	Inside leg:
Collar:	Height:

EMPLOYMENT HISTORY

Are you employed at present? YES/NO

If yes, please state your current employer's name, address, telephone and type of business:

Reason for wishing to leave?:

Have you previously worked in a position which involved dealing with the public and providing them with a service? YES/NO

If yes, please state your employer, name, address, telephone, type of business and your reason for leaving:

Job 1:   Job 2:

REFERENCES

Please give two employment references:

1

2

May we contact the above individuals/companies
after interview?   YES/NO

Have you worked for the company before? YES/NO

If yes, please state position and reason for leaving:

Do you have any close relatives who are employed by the company?
YES/NO

If yes, please state their position and department:

QUALIFICATIONS

Do you have any qualifications which are directly related to the
job you are applying for? YES/NO

If yes, please state ....

Subject: Qualification: Grade: Issuing body:

Please list any other qualifications below (e.g. degrees).

Subject: Qualification: Grade: Issuing body:

MEDICAL

Please give details of any illnesses you have suffered within the last 5 years and any current medical conditions:

Please state below your main reasons for applying for this job and what you think you could offer to our company:

I declare that the information on this application is correct. If employment is offered to me, it will be conditional on the receipt of satisfactory references.

Signature: Date:

• When completed please return this form to the PERSONNEL DEPARTMENT and attach 2 passport sized photographs to the top right hand corner.

Please indicate below your ethnic group. (This information will not be considered as part of your application and will be used solely to monitor the effectiveness of the company's equal opportunities policy.)

— White   — Chinese
— Afro-Caribbean   — Other
— Asian   (please specify) _____

Figure 6.2   A sample application form

How to tackle selection tests

The employment selection test has been around in the form we recognise today since the 1950s. This form of assistance with the recruitment process tends to wax and wane in fortune, sometimes being in fashion and sometimes out, but you are bound to encounter it from time to time. An understanding of tests and how they work can help you succeed at the selection level.

Understanding the purpose of selection tests

Two schools of thought apply to selection tests. One group believe in the scientific approach that all successful employees fit a pattern in their mental make up and behaviour. Therefore, once a successful model has been established all others who fit that model will also make a good employee. Other employers, however, simply use them as a filter. In other words, someone who cannot pass an elementary test must be totally unsuitable as any kind of employee and this is a very good way of reducing the number of employees to pass on to the next stage. Another school of thought believes that selection tests only benefit the companies who devise and sell them.

Whatever your opinion of selection tests it is very important not to degrade or dismiss them. Even if they seem silly or even childish they are a hurdle and a hurdle which you must pass. While most employers rate selection tests as low down on the priority scale the fact is that if you don't pass the selection test you cannot usually pass on to the next stage, and there are usually no second chances.

In this section we will look at some of the main types of selection test and how to tackle them. Your selection test may be given as separate tests, or you may find that several types of test are all rolled up into one test, so always be prepared for the unexpected.

Multiple choice selection tests

A multiple choice selection test is one where you are asked a series of questions and must choose the most appropriate answer. You may have encountered this type of test before. The principles are exactly the same in a job application.

A multiple choice test is conducted in order to allow applications to be sorted automatically, or allow certain applicants to be selected, or allow applicants to be compared. It is often used as a screen.

- Read the instructions carefully. There may be four or five answers.
- Read the questions carefully. There may be trick questions.
- There may be two correct answers. Unless it positively says there is only one correct answer then you should feel free to mark two or more, if appropriate.
- In case of questions with no right or wrong answer, such as personality questions, the answer you first think of is usually the best answer to choose.

Written selection tests

A written selection test is very much like a school examination. Normally you will be required to answer one or more questions, within a set time limit, under exam conditions.

- Read the questions very thoroughly before starting. The question may not actually be what it at first appears. It may have been purposely designed to catch out those who rush rather than read.
- Allocate the available time to each of the questions, if there is more than one. Try to avoid leaving any questions unanswered since, if short of time, you will receive more credit for answering all the questions partly rather than just some of the questions fully.
- Plan out your answer briefly before you start to write.
- Keep your answer well structured and your answer legible. Readable handwriting is a useful skill in most businesses.
- Concise answers are usually best. Unless a word limit is set, which is unlikely, try to keep your answers short but complete.

Psychometric tests

The purpose of a psychometric test is to compare an individual with a standard profile of a suitable employee as defined by test standards. They come in varying types. General ability tests measure verbal, numerical or comprehension skills. Specific ability tests rate skills such as keyboarding or language skills. Personality tests monitor for such factors as honesty, or whether the applicant has an introvert or extrovert personality. A further type of test (the psychodynamic test) observes an individual's reaction to a given situation.

It is not a good idea to try to outwit psychometric tests, since they are often designed to identify applicants who seek to do this. It is also often the case that selecting the answer which seems most obvious when you read the question is actually the right answer so far as you are concerned.

■ Read the instructions carefully. They can vary greatly from test to test and there may also be a trick element.

■ Manage your time properly. If there are 15 minutes and 30 questions to answer then, obviously, you should try to devote no more than 30 seconds to each answer.

■ Try to avoid leaving questions unanswered. If you have to, go through and answer the easier ones first before returning to the trickier ones.

■ In psychometric tests with multiple choice answers don't just tick any answer in questions to which you do not know the answer hoping that, for example, this should give you at least a one-in-four chance of getting the answer right. Often in psychometric tests there are no right or wrong answers and choosing an answer completely at random might identify you as an unsuitable candidate.

Finally, do try to take psychometric tests seriously, no matter how ridiculous the questions can sometimes appear. Your potential employer obviously does take them seriously or they wouldn't be used. In many ways, the use of psychometric tests reveals a great deal about the personality of your potential employer or personnel manager.

Practical selection tests

Practical selection tests normally test for skills which you will use in your day-to-day employment. Most usually, although they are not restricted solely to this area, they test what might also be known as trade skills. For example, if you are applying for a job as a typist you may be asked to type (or more likely wordprocess) a letter. If you are applying for a job as a beautician you may be asked to give a beauty treatment. Tests of this type are being used increasingly in the recruitment process as they provide a very real indication of an applicant's ability.

■ Always expect a practical selection test if your job involves the application of practical skills. Don't be caught out!

■ Ask if your practical skills are likely to be tested. Many employers prefer not to give prior notice, although if you ask you are unlikely to be misled. This will give you useful extra time to prepare.

■ If asked to undertake a test complete the assignment in exactly the same way as you would in your normal working environment. This will give the most realistic and also most professional representation of your ability.

■ If anything is unclear, ask. For example, if the job you do can be undertaken in several different ways, or different schools of thought govern how it should be done, ask what the employer's preferred practice is.

■ Offering to give a practical demonstration of your skills at interview can help tip the balance in your favour, where the employer has several equally suitable applicants to choose from.

Physical selection tests

You may occasionally encounter physical selection tests as part of a job application process. Such tests are rarely designed to test physical fitness. They are more likely designed to test manual skills, physical dexterity, mental dexterity or, in many cases, skills to which they seem totally unconnected such as organisational or leadership skills.

A typical example of a physical selection test is being formed into a team with other applicants, being given a number of items such as planks, ropes and barrels, and then being asked to ford an imaginary river. Many physical tests involve a variation on this theme, either on a larger or smaller scale.

■ Listen carefully to the instructions you are given. They may not be written down, which is intentional. Also listen carefully to any briefings you may have been given before the test began.

■ Most tests involve an element of make believe (for example, fording the imaginary river). However, try to actually visualise yourself in the situation. This will make solving it that much easier.

■ Look for catches and/or hidden shortcuts. These are a common feature of all tests of this type.

■ If the test involves forming a team propose yourself as team leader although in doing this try to let other people contribute to the team effort.

■ If you are working as part of a team and you don't, for whatever reason, become team leader make sure that you don't hide behind other people, or let them take over entirely. Make sure you contribute to the joint effort. If you don't it will be noticed and will almost certainly render you unsuitable.

Handwriting analysis

Handwriting analysis is becoming a more popular form of character analysis used as a form of selection test. It is more common in some countries, such as France. There is very little you can do to prepare for such a test. If asked to give a sample of handwriting then try to keep your writing as normal as possible, since a noticeable change in your writing style may lead the graphologist to believe you have either an erratic personality or have deliberately been trying to mislead them.

Role-playing games

The role-playing game is very popular. It is particularly common in types of jobs that involve selling, or in those which involve customer contact. If you are applying for this type of job then always be prepared for this type of test.

Again, always take this type of test entirely seriously. The interviewer is almost certainly likely to be familiar and comfortable with this type of selection test. So, even if the average man or women in the street would find it strange, they almost certainly will not.

Here are some tips:

■ If unclear about the role-playing situation ask for an explanation.

■ If offered time to prepare always accept it. It will show a sensible approach and you will not gain any points for turning the opportunity down.

■ If preparation time is not offered, but you feel you need it, then ask for it. It is unlikely you will be marked down for asking for this thinking time.

■ Deal with the situation as you feel you would deal with it, rather than as you feel you should. Even if you handle the situation badly you will at least come across as sincere.

■ Really try to envisage yourself in the situation.

■ Never be tempted to make jokes, or give any indication that you don't take the role-playing situation seriously.

■ Try to think one step ahead. Be ready for the interviewer to change tack, or throw in unexpected problems.

Examples of typical role-playing situations you might encounter

The sales situation

Likely situation: The interviewer plays a customer, the interviewee plays the part of a salesman or women who has to sell him or her the product in question.

How to handle: Unless you feel you know a better strategy, run through the chief benefits that your product can offer to your customer.

The complaining customer situation

Likely situation: The interviewer plays a customer, while the interviewee plays the part of a company representative. Usually the situation starts with the customer making an enquiry, which then deteriorates into a complaint.

How to handle: Try to give a logical explanation to each of the customer's concerns. If you cannot give an explanation, say that you will find out. Always try to defuse a complaining situation and do not let it turn into an argument.

The emergency situation

Likely situation: The interviewer plays the part of a colleague at work, with the interviewee playing the part of a colleague, boss or supervisor. A problem arises.

How to handle: Stay cool, calm and collected. Obtain a full explanation from the employee then issue step-by-step instructions on how to handle it.

How to write a great job application letter

Quite often when applying for your job you will need to write a formal application letter. This applies whether you are writing a letter in response to an advertised vacancy, or whether you are making a speculative approach to an employer. The application letter can make all the difference to the success of your application. Even if you are asked for a CV, and even if an application form is to be completed, this letter can make all the difference. It gives the personnel officer an extra reason for reading your CV and application form and helps your application to stand out.

What is the purpose of the application letter?

There are two main purposes to an application letter. The first is to provide the employer with the information they need to consider whether you are suitable for the job. The second is to show that you can organise and present information in a coherent way.

It is important to consider both these purposes when preparing your letter. Many applicants fall down in their applications by neglecting one if not both of these considerations. Sometimes even applicants who excel by means of their qualifications and experience fail to present this information well, while employers increasingly use presentation as a way of filtering out applications.

What an application letter must be

You should aim to make your application letter:

- Concise. One A4 page is ideal and two the maximum unless you have been asked for a large amount of information in the job advertisement.
- Clear, and well presented, to the best possible standard.
- Comprehensive. It should include all the information necessary to make a decision on whether you are suitable for the job. At the very least this should cover qualifications, experience and personal skills or suitability.
- Amicable. Avoid application letters which are cold and over-formal in tone. While you wouldn't want to be over-familiar, a warmer, more personal letter will always stand out.

Step-by-step to a great letter

These tips will help you to write a really great application letter:

- Always start with an opening paragraph that states what job you are applying for (if the job is advertised) or what sort of work you are looking for (if it is a speculative application).
- In the second paragraph give brief personal details, such as your age and brief details of your background.
- In the next paragraph say what job you are doing now and what level you have reached in it. If your current job is not directly relevant to the job you are applying for then explain why you want to change. If you have done a job in the past that is directly relevant then say so.

- Always say something about your experience, especially any that is directly relevant to this job.

- Say why you are qualified to do this job. Refer to any special qualifications. If you are not qualified 'on paper' then refer to any experience which you think qualifies you to do this job.

- Say why you think you are suitable for this type of job and give your main reason for wanting this job.

- Do not just say that you would like the job because you would enjoy it, or that it will help your career. This does not always go down well with employers. A much better way of saying this is that, for example, you see the company or industry as an expanding and progressive one which offers both you and the employers involved in it good prospects for the future.

- Always offer to attend for interview. Use the closing paragraph of the letter to do this. Offer any date, time or place. You can sort out the minor details once the interview has been offered, even if some dates are unlikely to be convenient.

Concerning presentation, you can either type, wordprocess or handwrite your application letter. Whichever method you use it must be clear and very well presented. Use blue or black ink on white, unlined paper. If you are applying for an advertised vacancy then check the application details carefully. If the advertisements asks for a handwritten letter of application, which some do, then always send a handwritten application rather than a typewritten one.

It is well worth taking time to write the best application letter you can. Once you have prepared a really good letter there is no reason why you cannot use it over and over again when applying to different employers. However, do make sure you check and change the relevant details in each letter so that it is customised to each job.

Ways to improve your letter

These tactics can be used to improve your job application letter:

- Read your letter through twice when you have finished. Once to check for mistakes in the presentation and once to check for factual mistakes in the content.

- Ask someone else to read your letter. This time ask them to read the job advertisement or job description first and then read your letter. Ask them if, firstly, it makes sense and, secondly, if they can think of any way it could be improved.

■ Write your letter and then leave it for 24 hours before rewriting it and sending it off. It is surprising how many more things you can then think of to include, and how easy it is to recognise and delete duplicated or unnecessary information.

■ Try to shorten your letter to around half its original length. You will probably find that you lose very little factual information but the result is a letter which is much easier for the employer to read.

The following are five common faults in job application letters:

1 Spelling mistakes and corrections. Never send a letter with a mistake or a correction.

2 Typed letters when handwritten letters are asked for and vice versa.

3 Inappropriate stationery, such as illustrated notelets and letters written in felt tip pen. Always use ink or a ballpoint pen.

4 Letters not addressed to anyone, or addressed to the wrong person.

5 Letters that are too formal, or too informal. Take some time to think about which approach is just right

Figures 6.3 and 6.4 illustrate some sample application letters.

How to organise a telephone application

The telephone has become common place as a tool in making a job application today. Although some applications still do not involve the use of the telephone there are, conversely, some other jobs that can only be applied for by telephone. If this is the case it is important to think how you can best make the use of the telephone in the application procedure.

The advantages of the telephone are that it is quick, and only a voice communication. The disadvantage is that it is only a partial form of communication. You cannot communicate by means of facial expressions and body language which can add so much to the meaning of a conversation.

Telephone calls can be used in two ways. In some cases they are the only way of getting the job. Most usually, however, they are used as a screen in that only those who pass the telephone interview or screening are allowed to proceed to the next stage. Telephone interviews are sometimes described as informal chats, although this is seldom a good way to approach them.

John Black
11 Any Road
Anytown AY50 1AB
Tel.0000 000 0000
1 December 199x

Mrs Sarah Smith
The Restaurant
PO Box 6000
Anytown AY1 1AB

Dear Mrs Smith

I should like to apply for the position of Restaurant Manager with The Restaurant as advertised in 'The Anytown News', 30 January.

I am 22 years old and have worked in the hotel and catering industry since leaving school when I commenced my training as a commis waiter with the Chez Nous restaurant group in London. At the moment I am employed as a waiter in the Ports of Call Restaurant in Manchester.

I am fully experienced in all aspects of a restaurant waiting and I have also obtained my NVQs at Levels 1, 2 and 3 in Food and Drink Service. I also run the restaurant in the manager's absence, controlling and supervising a team of up to eight waiters and waitresses.

I would very much like to obtain a position in your restaurant as I feel that it would be a job which would use my skills and experience to date to the full. I appreciate the friendly yet professional standards of service that operate in your restaurant and feel confident that I would be able to meet these standards and also integrate well with the restaurant team.

I enclose my CV for your consideration and would be very pleased to attend for interview if required.

Yours sincerely

John Black

Figure 6.3   A sample application letter applying for a job which has been advertised

John Black
11 Any Road
Anytown AY50 1AB
Tel.0000 000 0000
1 December 199x

The Personnel Manager
City Hotels Group
PO Box 9000
Anytown AY1 1YZ

Dear Sirs

I am writing to ask if you currently have any vacancies for the position
of Restaurant Manager.

I am 22 years old and have worked in the hotel and catering industry
since leaving school when I commenced my training as a commis
waiter with the Chez Nous restaurant group in London. At the moment
I am employed as a waiter in the Ports of Call Restaurant in
Manchester.

I am fully experienced in all aspects of a restaurant waiting and I have
also obtained my NVQs at Levels 1, 2 and 3 in Food and Drink
Service. I also run the restaurant in the manager's absence, controlling
and supervising a team of up to eight waiters and waitresses.

I would very much like to obtain a position in your restaurant as I feel
that it would be a job which would use my skills and experience to
date to the full. I appreciate the friendly yet professional standards of
service that operate in your restaurant and feel confident that I would
be able to meet these standards and also integrate well with the
restaurant team.

I enclose my CV for your consideration and would be very pleased to
hear if you have any vacancies for which I might be suitable.

Yours faithfully

John Black

**Figure 6.4   A sample application letter making a
speculative application to an employer**

When should you make a telephone application?

You should make a telephone application in preference to other forms of application in all these cases:

■ When it says so in the advertisement.

■ When there is a telephone number in the advertisement. You should at least call for further details, even if you later make a formal written application.

■ When there is any doubt about exactly what is required. For example, the job title is unclear or the job description in an advertisement is misleading.

■ When it is a particularly competitive situation. That is, when the employer is likely to receive hundreds of applications. A telephone call enables you to jump to the head of the queue and helps get your name remembered.

Preparations to make for a telephone application or interview

Calling immediately in response to an advertised job is almost always a mistake. It is sensible to allow yourself some time to think through the process and decide exactly what you want to say. It is quite acceptable to make some notes before calling and, in particular, make a list of key points which you would like to get across, such as:

■ Make sure you know exactly who you want to talk to.

■ Have as much information as possible ready.

■ Have your CV, all documents and the ad in front of you.

■ Make the call when you will not be disturbed, and in a quiet room.

■ Make a list of any questions you would like to ask. In fact, make a list in any case. You are very likely to be asked if you have any questions and should have some ready. It will allow you to prolong the interview and stand a better chance of standing out from the other applicants.

■ Have a CV ready to fax off immediately at the end of the interview if you are asked or if things go well. Don't call with an out-of-date CV which you will then have to hurry to update.

Making a success of telephoned applications

A telephoned application offers a good chance to shorten and simplify the application procedure. Indeed, this is why many employers use the technique. This does not mean it should not be treated as seriously as a written application. Here are some pointers which will help your telephoned application run more successfully:

■ Call at the right time. Times may be specified by the employer. If not, avoid obvious lunchtimes, although it is always difficult to tell what these might be. Avoid first thing Monday morning and last thing Friday afternoon if possible.

■ Always speak to the right person. Don't discuss the matter with anyone else in the hope they will relay the information as they probably won't.

■ If the person you need to speak to isn't available or is otherwise engaged don't leave a message for them to call you back. They may be more than willing to, but it doesn't allow you time to prepare for the call.

■ Always say which job you are applying for, as there may be more than one.

■ Go through your personal details and education briefly.

■ Focus on your work experience and why this is relevant to the job you are applying for.

■ Say why you think you are right for the job, and what you can offer to the post.

■ Don't do all the speaking. Allow the interviewer time to speak and address any of their questions.

■ The telephone interview is a two-way process. Listen to the impression the interviewer seems to be getting and adjust your approach accordingly.

■ Offer to send your CV and if your offer is accepted fax it immediately. Ask for the number so that, if possible, it reaches the interviewer's office rather than being sent somewhere else within the organisation.

Even if the interview doesn't go well be pleasant and polite and send your CV anyway (unless the interview was clearly a disaster). Other jobs may become available for which you would be more suitable and you may have to talk to the same person again.

Here are five common faults in telephone applications:

1 Speaking to the wrong person. Never leave a message, or begin explaining why you are right for the job to the secretary, rather than the personnel manager!

2 Not getting over the most important points of your application, such as your experience and qualifications.

3 Not getting, or making, an opportunity to say why you are right for the job.

4 Not listening to what the other person is saying, especially important questions which they ask you to which they must have answers if your application is to proceed.

5 Not following up any unanswered questions, because the conversation has moved on to other things. This may give the impression that you are being evasive.

How to make a telephone call: handling the informal chat

An informal chat is not a telephoned application as such. It is merely a telephone call made to a prospective employer who is advertising a vacancy to discuss the vacancy in question. Many job advertisements now contain the phrase: 'Please telephone for an informal chat'. This has proved to be an effective way of both screening unsuitable applications and identifying the best applicants. It also saves the employer time and money in sifting written applications. An informal chat can be used to increase your chances of finding the most suitable job, if it is approached correctly.

The pros and cons of the informal chat are the following:

Pros:

■ The informal chat helps get your name remembered.

■ It saves you time, filtering out jobs which you are unsuitable for.

■ It helps you gather extra information about the job, which you can use to tailor your application.

Cons:

■ Badly handled informal chats can prejudice your application. If you come across badly, for some reason, your application may be rejected as a result.

An informal chat should be approached in the following way:

■ Make a list of points you would like to make before calling.

■ Make sure you speak to the right person. Call at what are likely to be the most convenient times. Don't leave a message.

■ Try to get your approach just right. Remember that an informal chat is usually just that – informal. A friendly and personal approach is usually best. In any case it should be less formal than a formal telephoned application.

■ As you're speaking, make a list of points that the employer or interviewer mentions. About, for example, what the job involves or what type of person they are looking for. Incorporate all these points in your application. Also recap on your answers to any questions they ask you when submitting a written application.

How to make an application in person

The requirement to make a job application in person is presently the exception rather than the rule. In some countries where it is more common than others it is known as a 'walk in-interview'. It is, however, becoming more widely found since it saves the employer time and money in sifting applications. It is particularly appropriate for jobs which involve customer contact since the employer can follow the old adage that 'first impressions count', and may even select an applicant on that basis.

For a personal application or walk-in interview a time and place will normally be stated in the job advertisement and an open invitation issued to all suitable applicants to come along. Here are some pointers to help you succeed with this type of application:

■ If a telephone number is given call in advance. It may be possible to arrange an individual appointment which avoids the uncertainty of queuing for an interview. (A common problem at walk-in interviews.)

■ Try to arrive at the beginning of the event. The interviewers are always more receptive then.

■ Prepare for a walk-in interview in exactly the same way as you would any other interview.

■ Dress and personal appearance is particularly important at this type of event. Try to choose something that is appropriate to the job for which you are applying. If unsure, wear something smart.

■ Ascertain what is the purpose of this event. Is it to appoint candidates to a job? Or is it merely a screening event which will lead to a formal application? The latter is normally the case. Ask if unclear. If appointments are being made at the event treat the process as a normal job application. If they are not, make your one and only objective being placed onto the shortlist.

Finally, talk to other applicants at such events. As a jobseeker you will get very few other opportunities to do so. Use the opportunity to the full. Chat to the other applicants about other job opportunities, leads they know of, application techniques they have found useful (or which have proved failures).

Following up your application: getting your name noticed

Following up your application can often make the difference between being offered the job you want and not being offered it. Most particularly, in the case of positions where several equally able applicants are shortlisted – a common occurrence nowadays – it can be the deciding factor. You should always aim to follow up all job applications you make unless, after the initial stages, the job is clearly not for you and you are clearly not right for the job.

■ A note of thanks is appropriate after most interviews. It helps get you remembered, even if the courtesy isn't appreciated. (It normally will be.)

■ If you later think of, or obtain, any information which you think might reinforce your application send it on. A case in point here are references received after the initial application.

■ Telephone to follow up all applications and other letters you send in connection with a job. There is always the chance they might not have been received. Most importantly, however, names of applicants who do this tend to stand out.

■ Also follow up unsuccessful applications. This can reveal useful clues about what not to do next time.

Case studies

Following up rejected applications leads to eventual success

Alison Andrew had applied for several jobs without success and had no idea where she was going wrong. She decided to make a serious effort to find out. She telephoned the personnel officers of several companies she had unsuccessfully applied to and asked to discuss her application. Only one declined, the others were willing to discuss her applications and one was particularly helpful. She told Alison that they had automatically rejected her application because she hadn't explained two periods of unemployment in the CV. Alison amended her CV, explaining the reasons for the unemployment were that her previous employers had gone out of business. Shortly after, Alison was offered a job.

Exploiting the invitation to an informal chat

Mike Griffiths knew that the vacancy he spotted in the local evening paper was the right job for him. The advertisement asked applicants to apply in writing for the trainee pub manager's position, but also invited those interested to call the existing trainee manager for an informal chat. Michael telephoned and found he had a lot in common with the current trainee manager, had an opportunity to ask lots of questions, express his interest in the job and even suggest his own ideas for how the pub could be run! At the interview the current trainee manager was on the interview panel. As a result Mike felt much more confident and feels certain this helped him get the job.

Summary

■ Before applying, always stop to consider what (or who) the employer is looking for.

■ Dissect the application form carefully. It can provide a great deal of information about how it should be handled.

■ Always be ready for selection tests.

- Regard letters of application as an opportunity to sell yourself, not an unwanted chore. Use the opportunity they present to the full.
- Both telephoned and personal applications, and informal chats, are becomingly increasingly popular. Realise that they are essentially conducted to be more convenient for the employer, but you can exploit them to your own advantage.

7 | WINNING AT THE INTERVIEW

What is the aim of an interview?

In most cases an interview is a confirmatory process rather than entirely a selection process. Nowadays, most employers do not have the time and resources to interview every single applicant for a job. In almost all cases a shortlist is made of applicants who are probably suitable, based upon information supplied in the earlier stages of their application. An interview is conducted merely to confirm suitability or to select the optimum individual for the post concerned.

This has two important implications, which you should bear in mind. Firstly, being invited to interview is an indication that you are almost certainly suitable for the job. Thus the onus to prove this is not as important as it was at the application stage. The onus should be on performing well at interview. Secondly, you are now in a competitive situation with other applicants, rather than the job specification itself, which you already comply with. Hence, anything you can do to differentiate yourself from other applicants can increase your chances of getting the job considerably. Small details make all the difference.

Preparing for the interview

There is a great deal you can do before the day of the interview that can actually increase your chances of getting the job. Many of these are practical steps that few applicants consider. They can help make the occasion of the interview itself run more smoothly, and also present a more professional, more organised impression to the employer.

Find out where the interview is and how long it is going to take you to get there. Being late is one of the worst things you can do. If for some reason you are unavoidably late then telephone and say so. It may be possible to reschedule your interview for later.

Take some copies of your letter, CV and application form. You can then re-read these just before the interview to make sure that everything you say agrees exactly with what you have written. If you haven't been asked for a CV so far then take some copies of this so you can hand them out at interview. This will show you are well organised and have planned ahead.

Plan what you are going to wear well before the interview. This is covered in more detail in the next section.

Find out how many people will be conducting the interview. This will prevent you from being caught out by, for example, a panel interview (of two or more people). You can telephone beforehand to ask if you want to check on this.

Find out if you might be asked to do any tests or assessments at the interviews. For example, some employers might ask you to write an essay or take a multiple choice aptitude test. Others might expect you to take part in a role-play exercise where, for example, you take the part of a staff member and the interviewer takes the part of a customer, or perhaps even a customer making a complaint. Think beforehand how you will tackle these tests if they arise.

You might be asked to do a demonstration, particularly if your job involves a manual skill. For example, a guide might be asked to guide a tour, or a sports coach may be asked to coach a class. Be prepared just in case and also bring anything with you that you think you might need, such as personal tools or special clothing.

If your job involves any language ability then you should expect your ability to be tested. This may be assessed by a random question made in the appropriate language. It doesn't matter how well or badly you handle this as long as the ability you demonstrate concurs with the level of ability you have stated in your application.

Make a list of:

- ■ Questions you are likely to be asked and your likely answers.
- ■ Any points you wish to make during the interview. For example, about your experience or suitability for the job.
- ■ Questions you want to ask the interviewer.

While you wouldn't want to refer to your list during the interview it can help to make a list and take it with you. Just before you arrive for the interview go through your list and commit the main points to memory.

Try a mock interview with a friend acting as interviewer. Try the likely interview questions given later in this section. It is also worth going for a few interviews for jobs you are not especially interested in, just to develop your skills. You'll often find that when the pressure to succeed is off you handle the interview much better and will be able to pick up many tips you can use at an interview for a job that you really want.

Dress and appearance

Give some thought to what you are going to wear at the interview, well in advance. Dress and appearance count for a great deal nowadays and going to the interview with the most suitable appearance can make a great deal of difference to the outcome. At worst, the employer could make a hire-or-not judgement based on your appearance. At the very least it could help sway a decision. Remember we live in a very image-conscious world.

■ Don't be too casual. Never wear jeans and T-shirts! The best things to wear are a suit (or at least a shirt and tie) for men, and a skirt and blouse, perhaps with a jacket, for women.

■ Unless you are going to an interview for a job where fashion sense is important (such as a fashion buyer) think in conservative terms when choosing what to wear. Brightly coloured clothing, for example, doesn't appeal to everyone.

■ Make sure your hair is neat and not overstyled. For men, above collar length hair is always the safest bet. There is still a lot of prejudice about men with very long hair, or women with very short hair for that matter. If you consider yourself an individualist then it is best to demonstrate your individualism once you have started the job, not at the interview!

■ Don't wear large amounts of jewellery. A simple ring is acceptable. Several rings, lavish necklaces and chains are not a good idea. Women should wear simple earrings. It's possible that the employer may be prejudiced against men wearing earrings.

■ If you are hoping to get a job that involves working with the public then pay special attention to this. The interviewer will assume that the way you dress at interview is the way you would like to dress at work. If you can choose an outfit that resembles, fairly closely, any corporate clothing that the employer's staff wear then this may help.

■ If you are travelling some distance to the interview take some toiletries with you so that you can 'freshen up' just before you get to the interview. It can also be a good idea to take a spare shirt, spare tights and so on with you so that you have something to change into, in case of unexpected accidents such as spills or ladders en route. It may seem unnecessary, but you will feel more relaxed about the interview.

■ Finally, before going into the interview, check your appearance at the very last minute.

Tackling the interview

Although preparation is important, it is what actually happens at the interview that will ascertain whether you get the job or not. So, it is a good idea to do what you can to help the interview go your way: don't sit there and let the interviewer do all the work. Make sure that you create opportunities to say what you want to say.

Here are some of the ways you can improve your interview handling technique:

■ It is very important to be on time! Try to get there about ten minutes before the interview starts.

■ Don't smoke, even if the interviewer says he or she doesn't mind. You won't be allowed to smoke while on duty in any case as most employers have completely banned smoking on their premises. Some employers even discriminate against smokers.

■ Greet the interviewer with a 'good morning' or 'good afternoon' as appropriate and shake their hand if offered.

■ Always sit confidently. Don't slouch in the chair.

■ Make eye contact with the interviewer when speaking to them. This builds up a rapport with the interviewer, and is also a good sign of honesty.

■ When you are asked a question never answer just 'yes' or 'no'. Fill in with a few background details too. As well as keeping the interview flowing in a more amicable manner this also shows that you have prepared well.

■ If you aren't sure what the interviewer is asking then ask them to explain the question. This is also a good technique to use if you need a little time to think of a good answer to the question.

■ Avoid criticising your present employer (or past employers too) even if you feel you have good reason to. Don't be tempted to reveal too much about the business of your current employers as this might be considered a breach of confidence – not a good quality in a prospective employee. Try to keep strictly to what your role was within the organisation.

■ Try to keep your answers fairly short, as long as you answer the question fully. If the interviewer looks bored, looks away, yawns and so on, then take it as a hint. Finish answering the question as soon as possible and wait for the next question!

■ Say what you mean rather than what you think the interviewer wants to hear. If you answer honestly then, even if you give a less-than-ideal answer, at least you will come across as an honest person which is a very important quality for most types of work.

■ Thank the interviewer afterwards. It is a minor courtesy but can make all the difference.

Dealing with panel interviews

A panel interview can be considered as any type of interview conducted before two or more interviewers, rather than just one. They are becoming more usual, as employers tend towards spreading the responsibility for recruitment amongst several individuals. Panel interviews typically consist of three members, although panels of up to seven interviewers are used in a small number of cases!

Most candidates find panel interviews daunting and, indeed, they should be considered as trickier to perform well in than one-to-one interviews. However, there are certain ways that you can increase your chances of success with a panel interview.

Pros and cons of panel interviews include the following:

Pros:

■ There is a greater chance that you will get on well with at least one of the interviewers, if not them all.

■ It is likely that a panel decision will be made as a result of a panel interview. Panel decisions tend to go in favour of middle-of-the-road candidates with all round ability which, by the law of averages, you are most likely to be.

Cons:

■ The environment of a panel interview can be intimidating.

■ It can be difficult to retain your composure, as different questions are fired from different angles, and on different topics.

Here are some pointers for handling a panel interview:

■ Forewarned is forearmed. Try to find out if a panel interview is likely and, if so, who the panel will be consist of.

■ Accept that panel interviews are unfair to the candidate. They are meant to be, by placing you under extreme pressure. It is best to accept this rather than feeling disgruntled, which will come across in the interview. Instead try to give the impression that you welcome the opportunity to talk to as many people as possible.

■ At the start of the interview, at the introductions, listen carefully to who each panel member is and what their job is within the organisation in question. This will enable you to anticipate the questions they are likely to ask.

■ One member of the panel will normally be appointed as the Chairman (or woman). Make sure you identify who this is, if you are not told. Your replies to the main questions can be directed to them. Replies to questions from other panel members should be directed to those members. When the conversation returns to more general matters, again direct your replies to the Chair.

■ Maintain eye contact with the Chair for most of the time, but also maintain occasional eye contact with other members of the panel.

■ Avoid warming to the most open and friendly member of the panel (there usually is one) at the expense of ignoring the most hostile one. Remember that panel members often have an equal say in the eventual decision even if they do not take an equal part in the questioning.

■ If given the opportunity to ask questions, direct them to the Chair.

■ Stay neutral if petty arguments or disagreements break out between members of the panel, for example on questions to be asked or the answers to them.

■ At the close of the interview, try to direct your thanks to each member of the panel. If the panel is too large direct your thanks and closing remarks to the Chair.

Dealing with group interviews

A group interview is very different from a panel interview. It is a situation where a large number of applicants meets with, usually, a smaller number of interviewers. The aim of the interview is to develop a conversation from which the interviewers can assess each interviewee.

A group interview is most usually used for screening purposes. That is, to identify candidates who will be invited to submit an application or progress to an individual interview. It is not usually used for the purposes of appointing an applicant.

■ Recognise that the purpose of a group interview is to pass to the next stage. Devote yourself to this, rather than trying to secure the job as such.

■ Aim to participate fully in the discussion. Anticipate questions that are directed to you, but also make sure that you answer a significant number of questions that are directed to the group as a whole.

■ Be ready to give a talk about yourself to the group, be asked to give a speech on a given subject (for example a subject in the news), or for your group to conduct a debate or group discussion. All these techniques are very widely used in group interviews.

■ If a group discussion is launched appoint yourself as leader of the group wherever possible. You should act as a Chair in this respect, organising the discussion and giving each member a chance to speak, before formulating a group consensus. This is the surest way to progress to the next stage of the application procedure. Don't, however, dominate the proceedings. Give other members of the group a chance to contribute.

Answering interview questions

The majority of interviews are essentially questions-and-answers sessions, rather than conversations as such. Even an interview that is ostensibly described as a chat will usually consist largely of questions and answers. It is useful to remember this for two reasons. Firstly, you should aim to develop your question answering technique. Secondly, you should try to anticipate likely questions. The advantage of this is that since the range of questions that is asked at most interviews is quite limited you can, with a little effort, become proficient at answering interview questions.

Here are some questions you could be asked at interview and some tips on how to handle them. Of course, you wouldn't say anything that was untrue but there is a lot you can do to answer the questions in a way which the interviewer would like you to handle them. You will find it useful to prepare outline answers to each of these questions, as it relates to each job you are applying for, before each interview you attend.

What does your present job involve? Give a brief report of what you do. A 'day in the life of' report is an easy way to do this.

What responsibilities do you have in your present job? Try to stress things that you are responsible for, or projects that you have contributed directly to, especially things that are directly related to customer service.

Would you like to tell us about yourself? The important thing here is to be brief. Focus on your education and any jobs you've done and say a few words about your background.

Why do you want this job? You must always be ready for this question. We've already given you some ideas in the section on filling in application forms, so be sure to have an answer ready.

Do you know much about our company? Do avoid having to say no. Try and find out a little bit about it beforehand so you can give a few basic details. If possible, go to the library and do a little background research on the prospective employer. If it is a large public company they may have an annual report and accounts (available free of charge if you telephone the head office and ask) which will give you a useful insight into what this company does and the way in which they work. If your potential employer is a local authority or a voluntary agency they may have publicity material which they can send you. If you have time, try and visit the place (whether a pub or sports centre or whatever) where you will be actually working so you can see exactly what it is like.

Why do you want to work for us? This question is quite different from 'why do you want this job'. You should say why you have chosen this particular employer. A good tip here is to try to find out about something they are known for.

What do you see yourself doing in five years time? Be honest. If there is nothing else you can think of a good answer is to say that you hope to be in the same line of work, but in a more senior position.

What do you most enjoy about your work? You could give many possible answers to this question. However, for a job that involves customer contact, for example, you could try to highlight a liking for serving the customer to the highest possible standard.

What does your husband/wife/boyfriend/girlfriend think about your applying for this job? It always makes good sense to discuss jobs you apply for with your partner before you apply for them as it is an increasingly popular tactic for interviewers to ask this type of question. Take some time to work out a good answer beforehand.

What do you think the drawbacks would be of working as a ...? Take some time to think about what the job involves and also the drawbacks. (If you can think of at least three or four drawbacks then this will show that you have really thought about what you are doing.) Obviously it depends on the job involved but key drawbacks to consider are unsocial hours, irregular hours, working away from home, or working in a hazardous environment.

More tips for succeeding at interview

Here are some more tips for succeeding at interview:

■ Always check and double-check the requirements which the employer has stated he or she requires in the advertisement or job particulars. Expect to be asked how you fit those requirements, and make some decisions on how exactly you are going to illustrate this.

■ Use any methods that are available for finding out as much as possible about the employer and the vacancy before the interview. Do your own research and take advantage of invitations to an informal chat.

■ Don't let the interview consist of the interviewer asking questions and you answering. Make a list of points you want to raise beforehand, and do everything possible to try to raise them. Most interviewers are more than happy to let you do this, although won't necessarily make time unless you suggest it.

■ Try to cover every eventuality but if you really can't answer a particular question say so. This is often better than giving an inadequate answer, or saying anything that comes into your head. Some interviewers ask *unanswerable questions* to test your reaction and don't expect an answer to them anyway.

Exercises

Devise your own personal interview preparation plan. Make a list of preparations you might make:

1 A week before the interview.
2 The day before the interview.
3 Just before arriving for the interview.

Case study: Sue Choi takes the employer's point of view

Sue Choi uses an innovative strategy when preparing for any job interviews she attends. She sits down with the original job advertisement and any other information she can obtain about the employer and creates a profile of the ideal candidate for this job. She then writes a list of questions which she would ask candidates if she were the interviewer. She then replaces his jobseeker's hat and devises the best way of answering these questions. On several occasions Sue feels that this strategy has helped her to identify likely questions which later arose in the interview and thus she was able to answer them more effectively.

Summary

- Understand the aim of an interview both generally, and as it relates to your particular application.
- Always prepare for every interview individually.
- Have a strategy for tackling interviews on the day.
- Be ready for non-standard interview formats, such as panel interviews.
- Interview questions are notoriously predictable. Always devise answers to the most likely ones. (Although it's perfectly acceptable to modify them to suit each individual case.)

8 | WINNING IN YOUR CURRENT WORKPLACE

In this chapter we will follow the theory that the best job is the one you already have. In other words, when seeking a better position with better prospects there is much more to be gained by staying within the organisation where you are currently employed than changing to a completely different one. While this strategy will not suit everyone keen to win in the jobs market it is certainly an approach that should be considered carefully.

This chapter will contain practical advice on how to secure promotion within the same organisation as a viable alternative to switching to another employer. The chapter will help you ascertain if good promotion prospects exist or not, and decide the best way of securing the position you seek.

Understanding the structure of your organisation

The first thing you must do in seeking to win in the promotion game is to understand the structure of your organisation. Only by understanding the structure and your position within it can you ascend through that structure to reach the positions you really want.

Take some time to examine the structure of the organisation you currently work for. If necessary, research into it a little further. Aim to understand how promotion takes place within your organisation.

The following questions should lead to some important discoveries about your current employer:

Is there room for promotion or not? As you move up the hierarchy the number of available positions normally reduces. Have you reached a point where the individuals whose positions you could be promoted to are unlikely to move on?

Does an organised promotional structure exist, or is it a shambles? Look at how other people have moved up the promotional ladder (or not). Ask older colleagues if they have followed an organised career path, or not.

Is promotion granted on time served or merit? In other words, do you have to work for promotion, or just wait?

Are certain qualifications required before you can progress? This is becomingly increasingly relevant nowadays. Must you obtain a particular qualification before you can even be considered for a promotion?

Is there an accelerated promotional system in place? If you have particular qualifications (such as a degree) is there a mechanism by which you can short-circuit the accepted methods of promotion? Are you able to use it?

Which promotional routes seem to be most common? Again, ask older colleagues and those who have been employed with this organisation longer than you how they – or others – rose up the ladder.

Does promotion normally occur within the same company, or to different sites/branches/subsidiaries? For example, would the next step on the ladder for you be a move to head office, or your own branch. In other words, do your prospects depend on development at another location of which you have little knowledge.

When you have answered these questions you will normally find that your organisation offers:

- Good prospects for promotion; or
- Bad prospects for promotion; or
- Unknown prospects for promotion.

This will help you decide whether to seek to remain within the same organisation or not.

Outside forces to consider

The next step in making a decision on the prospects within your organisation is to study what external forces might be at work. Although, in theory, achieving a promotion is as simple as serving a certain period of time, obtaining certain qualifications or performing well, it is rarely as simple as that in practice. Consider if any of the following forces are operating in your organisation:

Is nepotism at work? Are promotions given to favourites, regardless of ability? or friends and relatives? This is particularly the case in small and family businesses but even large-company employees should not ignore its influences.

Office politics. Is it necessary to know the right people, or play the game a certain way to secure a promotion? Are you able to lock into this system for your own benefit, or will it always conspire against you?

Dead men's shoes. Can promotion only be achieved when someone higher up in the hierarchy is promoted, leaves or retires (not necessarily dies)? This is less of a problem than it used to be, but can still be problematic in older or declining industries.

The glass ceiling effect. This term has been coined to explain a process by which women are unlikely to gain quick promotion (or even any promotion) simply because they are women. Such situations are still a problem even today and are even more difficult to cope with because most employers deny that such forces operate (hence the use of the descriptive term 'glass'). A similar situation can apply to ethnic groups, disabled people or mature employees, although discrimination applied to these groups is often less well disguised and easier to detect.

Is promotion bought? Do you need to buy your promotion with favours for others, or changes of policy or practice that you would not otherwise do? Remember, in these situations no money need change hands but your promotion may be very expensive in terms of favours and comprises.

Once you have considered the above points you will be in a much better position to decide if you should or should not seek promotion.

Deciding which post to aim for

Once you have decided to seek promotion within your organisation the next step is to decide which post to aim for.

EXERCISES

Make a list of all the jobs or job descriptions which you would like to do within your organisation. Include them all, from the very simplest to the most ambitious – such as Managing Director. At this stage, it does not matter whether they are easily obtainable, or seemingly unobtainable.

When you have made your list divide them up into:

■ Short-term objectives.
■ Medium-term objectives.
■ Long-term objectives.

For example:

■ Short-term objectives: Head of Northern Area Sales Team.
■ Medium-term objectives: Sales Manager.
■ Long-term objectives: Sales Director.

The jobs you should choose are almost certainly those which you have listed under the short-term route. By listing them under short term you have shown that you feel you are ready for this promotion. By listing jobs in long term you are admitting to yourself that you are not. If you do not feel ready for promotion now then it is unlikely that your employer will.

Of course, this is an ongoing situation. You might like to repeat it every six months or so. You should find that medium term become short term, long term become medium term, and new goals and ambitions enter the long-term list. It is also perfectly acceptable to change your list, as new situations develop.

You should now take each of the jobs in your short term list and screen them all in an attempt to find which job you should target in your promotional campaign. Ask yourself the following questions about each of the jobs on your list:

■ Would I enjoy this job?
■ Could I do this job?
■ Do I have the necessary qualifications and experience?
■ Who can teach me this job?
■ Who is the most influential person who can help me get this job?
■ What improvements would I bring to this job? How would I do it differently?
■ Is the pathway to this job open or barred?
■ Is this position a prime candidate for a promotion?

If the post has been occupied by many people in the last few years – to your knowledge – then it is fertile territory for the ambitious. If it has been held by the same person for many years then – unless they are about to retire or be sacked – it may not be. If you have not worked for this company for long, ask around. Glean what you can from long standing employees.

Finally, ask the question:

■ What is the most direct pathway into this job?

This is the most critical question of all.

You are now in a position to decide which job you are going to aim for in the promotional stakes. Write it down.

Setting a time limit

It is important to realise that the promotion game is an ever-fluid situation and it can change at short notice. It is therefore important to set a time limit on your activities. Six months is a sensible time limit in most organisations. If you have not made progress towards your new post within six months then repeat your process again and set a new target for promotion.

Also, if any of the following happen, repeat your search process again:

■ If someone else is appointed to your target post.

■ If your target post is changed in some way (especially if it ceases to exist of course).

■ If your company is taken over or merged. This may make fewer opportunities, or it may make more.

■ If the operating structure of your company is changed. For example, branches or departments are added, closed or merged.

How to plan a 'promotion campaign'

With a target in mind you can decide on how to develop a promotional campaign. The best way to think of this is that it should be organised as a campaign. This is, however, only for your own guidance and it is best not to let anyone else know exactly how you are targeting a job for promotion, especially not the current postholder, unless they are in a position to help you with your plans.

Here are some ways in which you can do this:

Enhance your profile. Aim to get noticed. You might do this by changing your appearance slightly, or simply become more involved in those activities and projects which normally aren't considered obligatory.

Let everyone know you are interested in promotion. This can be as simple as telling them. By announcing your interest in promotion you do not have to reveal the techniques you are using to go about it.

Get to know the current postholder. While this seems like an underhand act it is not necessarily the case. They may have plans to move on themselves, in which case you will have advance notice of the availability of their post. On the other hand if they have absolutely no plans to move on and are unlikely to be promoted you will know not to waste your time on trying to take over their post.

Learn what you can from the current postholder. Also learn about the work of their unit, division or department. This will not only prepare you for the job but show that you are interested.

Make contact with people who are in a position to put you into your chosen post. Find out who this is. It may be a head of department, the personnel manager, or even the managing director. Make sure they know that you are (a) available and (b) keen.

Make contact with people who you will be working with if you are promoted to the post. This includes people at a much lower level, as well as higher, and also outside contacts, such as suppliers.

Co-operate with these people as much as possible. Offer to work on joint projects, even if it is not strictly your responsibility and/or requires unpaid work.

Communicating with your employer

If you have followed the pointers in the previous section then those who are in a position to promote you should quickly become aware of your interest in progressing within the organisation. Don't expect, however, that these subtle means will be enough to achieve your objective. You may also need to use more obvious means to make your aims known. This can be achieved by communicating with your employer properly.

The secret here is to time your preparations and then your communications correctly. After several weeks of sending out messages that you are interested in a position you should then be able to progress to more direct communications:

- Find out who is responsible for making decisions on promotion.
- Find out who is responsible for handling applications.
- Find out whether you need to apply, or whether you will be selected. (A combination of both methods operates in many organisations, but do check.)
- Make it clear you are interested in promotion whenever suitable opportunities present themselves, such as meetings, seminars and even asides with colleagues or chance meetings in or out of work.
- Apply for suitable internal vacancies that arise. While following the promotional trail it is important not to neglect looking for and applying for any suitable internal vacancies that arise, such as vacant posts advertised within your own organisation. These may provide a better route to your chosen route or, in some cases, you may even find that the post you have been aiming for is advertised unexpectedly.

Things that get you noticed

Apart from operating your promotional campaign you will also find it helpful to demonstrate other skills that make others aware of your suitability for and interest in promotion. These are not necessarily skills which are directly related to the matter of being promoted. They are skills which you probably practice anyway in your day-to-day work. The secret, if there is one, is to make others aware that you possess these skills.

Effective management skills

Since, by definition, any job to which you are promoted involves some management or, at the very least supervisory skills, it is advisable to develop these skills where possible. Look for any courses that may be available. Look for opportunities to develop and practice your management skills, such as by standing in for someone at a higher level of responsibility.

Leadership skills

A leadership skill can usually be considered as the ability to lead others into activities or projects for which they have little or inadequate experience, and go on to produce a successful outcome. These are necessary for many positions to which you are promoted, especially in management. To demonstrate these skills volunteer for special projects, or offer yourself to lead a team in situations where teamwork is required.

Effective teamworking

Teamworking is currently very much a buzzword in the jobs market. Unless you plan to work for a very small company you will almost certainly be working as part of a team. Employers are strongly attracted to those who can demonstrate good team skills. It is recognised as producing a more productive as well as more harmonious working environment.

Collect evidence of teamworking skills, such as tasks or projects you have worked on which called for close teamwork. Volunteer to assemble or lead a team for a particular project. On a different level, evidence of competence in team sports is often highly regarded.

Developed business and personal skills

Well developed business and personal skills, as discussed earlier in this book, show that you are ready for promotion and that you have the basic tools to cope with a higher level of responsibility. Demonstrate these skills in your day-to-day work and also outside work where possible.

How to apply for an internally advertised vacancy

What is an internally advertised vacancy?

An internally advertised vacancy can be described as a job vacancy promoted by your current employer rather than another company and one which is advertised internally.

If a company advertises vacancies internally it normally means that they expect people who already work for the company to apply and also that they believe they stand a better chance of filling it this way. As a result internally advertised vacancies are some of the easiest types of promotion to get and if they include the type of job you would wish to do you should always apply for them.

Finding out about internally advertised vacancies

If you are interested in internally advertised vacancies you must first find out about them. This is not always easy, as there may be no official channels by which information can be obtained. Therefore:

■ Check to see if your company has a regular vacancy bulletin to advertise internally advertised vacancies. Or this information may be contained in a company newsletter.

■ Check to find out if any one person is responsible for handling these vacancies. There may be someone within your company who collates these vacancies but who does not actually publish them as such.

■ If none of the above apply decide by which method you can find out about these vacancies. It may be a matter of just talking to the right people and keeping your ear to the ground.

Applying for internally advertised vacancies

Once you have found out about the existence of internally advertised vacancies you will then need to decide whether you want to apply for them and, if so, apply for them as soon as possible. It is important to note that the procedure may differ from that which is appropriate for applying for external vacancies.

Find out well in advance what procedure should be followed. Do you have to lodge a formal application? Or do you simply have to talk to the right person. Once a vacancy arises, it may be too late to learn. In either case, lodge your application as soon as you learn about the vacancies. Internal vacancies are often filled much more quickly than external vacancies.

If you are required to follow a formal application procedure, as is usually the case in larger organisations, follow the advice given earlier in the book. If the procedure is informal deal with it in an informal way; all that may be necessary is to talk to the right person.

Important checks to make

Here are some important checks to make when considering internal vacancies:

■ Are the details of the job, and in particular the responsibilities, the same as for the current postholder? There may have been some changes to the job description.

■ Is it a new post? If so, exactly what is involved?

■ Are the employment terms the same? It is vital to check that the terms and conditions of the vacancy are the same. Employers sometimes create new posts in order to change (normally reduce) the terms and conditions of your employment. You will not normally find that the terms are better. Most likely they will be the same or less. If they are reduced then you must ensure that the additional benefits (e.g. pay and prospects) compensate for this.

■ What are the promotion prospects? In theory, they should be better than your current position, but this may not necessarily be the case.

How to impress at a promotion interview

Many if not all promotion posts require you to undergo an interview. It is important to realise that this is not just a formality. If an interview is convened then it tends to indicate that there are unanswered questions yet to be resolved about your suitability for the post. Never accept any assurances that such an event is just a formality.

It is also important to realise that the promotion interview must be conducted differently from that for the interview for a position for a new employer. These are the key differences:

■ The employer knows about you. They are going to ask fewer elementary questions. By the same token it isn't possible to elaborate on, for example, your experience as in a normal interview.

■ The employer knows about your failures as well as your successes. You cannot hide these and, in fact, they are very likely to be brought up at the interview.

■ Office politics can come into play. You may not get the job simply because your face does not fit, or you have made enemies at some point in the past.

■ There is often a bias against promoting. The employer knows that you can do your current job. They may doubt that you can do another. It also gives them the headache of finding someone to fill your post.

■ Outside candidates can have more of an advantage than you think. An old saying goes along the lines of better the devil you know than the devil you don't. So far as work goes employers often prefer a new broom.

Handling the promotion interview

The promotional interview should be handled rather differently from that for any other job. Here are some pointers:

■ It is still advisable to prepare details of your suitability, as regards skills, experience and qualifications. The person who is conducting the interview may not have this information to hand.

■ Do not be misled into considering that small talk about your current position is irrelevant – that especially regarding successes, failures and problems. Everything that is said at the interview is relevant. You may, in fact, be asked to explain your past actions.

■ Be sure to prepare clear reasons why you want this promotion. The question will almost certainly be asked and you should have more than one reason.

■ Be ready to talk about your plans for the new post. How will you develop the post? What changes will you make? Why? Be prepared to discuss these very specifically.

■ It is acceptable to make ambitious claims and proposals for the future, but you must be able to support them.

Likely promotional interview questions

One of the great difficulties of the promotional interview is that your past employment history is known, and often known personally by the person who is conducting the interview. If they do not know you personally do not believe that they will not have taken the time to find out. The questions are, therefore, more likely to be based upon your past employment history with your current employer rather than on more general issues. Here are some likely questions and pointers for handling them:

Why do you want promotion? It is acceptable to mention personal ambition, but try to mention how you feel you can contribute to the employer's business once you have been promoted.

What do you think you can contribute to the position? Not to be confused with your answer to the previous question. Try to be specific when covering this area. Try to give concrete examples of projects you think you could work on or even initiate.

What do you think the previous postholder did well/did wrong? Aim to give examples of both types of situation. It is acceptable to criticise the outgoing postholder, but try to be objective.

What changes do you intend to make? Again, try to give examples of changes or projects. Be ambitious but realistic, linking your aims and objectives with current policies.

What do you think is your best success to date? This question will almost certainly be asked. Prepare your answer, with several alternatives if possible. If you wish, it is usually acceptable to produce documents, charts and so on to support your explanation.

How do you think you could have handled such-and-such better? Always be ready for your failures – and there are sure to be some minor and major – to be brought forth for general discussion and direction. Be ready for this. Do not attempt to plaster over the cracks. The fact that such-and-such has been mentioned as a failure shows that those in charge definitely recognise it as a failure. The best course of action is to recognise it as a failure but show what you did to try and recover the situation. Also suggest what could be done to avoid a similar situation in future.

Case study: Charles exploits promotional opportunities

After working in the same post for five years Charles Evans had been looking for a position that offered him more responsibility and greater pay for several months. Despite various offers he never found a position with which he felt entirely happy. Charles decided to explore promotional opportunities with his current employer in more detail, an option which had not previously seemed possible. After implementing a promotional strategy Charles obtained a promotion to Branch Manager at a nearby branch. On reflection, Charles decided that lack of communication had been the reason why he had not secured a better position earlier. His employer merely assumed that employees were not willing to move branches and there was no official system for advertising internal vacancies. Charles made the implementation of an internal vacancy bulletin one of his aims in his new job.

Summary

- Always consider new posts with your current employer as equally valid routes to succeeding in the jobs market.
- Understand the promotional structure of your organisation.
- Have a strategy for dealing with promotion opportunities. Learn to spot the opportunities and the difficulties.
- Explore the opportunities for internally advertised vacancies, including those which aren't officially advertised.
- Understand the differences between a standard interview and promotional interview.

Part-time working is becoming increasingly common place in all kinds of industries. It offers many advantages to the employer, who can benefit from the increasing flexibility that part-time workers offer and, in many cases, lower costs too.

In the past, part-time working was often seen as a second-best option for many employees. Often, part-time jobs were only for those who were unable to find full-time jobs, or those with commitments that prevented them from working full-time, such as mothers with children. Slowly but surely this traditional image of the part-time job is changing and will continue to do so in future. While employers continue to be enthusiastic about part-time work, that enthusiasm is now being shared by employees who see part-time working opportunities as a way to win in the jobs market without the need to devote themselves to it full time.

Here are some pros and cons of part-time working.

Pros:

■ Part-time working offers greater flexibility to co-ordinate work or career with your personal life.

■ Part-time work opens up a greater variety of job choices.

■ You may be able to take several jobs, allowing you to work whatever weekly or monthly combination of hours you wish, and allowing you to learn and use many different and diverse skills.

■ Employers are more willing to employ you. It is usually much easier to get a part-time job.

■ It is a good way of getting extra experience and acquiring extra work skills to increase your employability in future.

Cons:

■ Part-time working often refers to lower status jobs. Career positions are less frequently offered on a part-time basis. This is changing, but only gradually.

- It is difficult to co-ordinate more than one job. There is a risk of overstretching yourself.
- Rates of pay can be poor.
- Working conditions and fringe benefits can be poor. Part-time workers are often denied benefits such as holiday pay, sick pay and staff concessions.

How to make a success of part-time working

Making a success of part-time working, or pursuing part-time jobs as a career, rather than just a source of occasional income, requires a degree of determination on the part of the employee. These pointers will show how to make part-time employment a career opportunity in its own right, rather than a second best option. Here are some points to consider:

- Choose part-time working for the benefits it offers (such as the ability to balance work and leisure) not as a second best option.
- Use a part-time job to acquire new skills, perhaps things that you have not considered doing before. These can be useful in the future.
- Look for employers who see part-timers as a valuable resource, not a way of obtaining cheap staff.
- Look for employers who offer flexibility to part-time workers. For example, those employers who offer the option to work when you want to work rather than enforcing fixed hours.
- Look for employers who offer the same or similar benefits to part-time workers as they do their full-time personnel.

Where to find part-time jobs

Advertised vacancies

A large proportion of part-time employment opportunities are advertised in some way. The most appropriate sources of advertisements are regional and local newspapers and free newspapers. Remember the following points:

- Use all possible advertised sources, so as to give yourself the best possible choice of jobs, on the best possible terms.

■ Never make an assumption about the hours, pay and conditions of an advertised part-time vacancy. No two part-time jobs are alike, and the conditions may be much better/worse than you expect.

■ Be selective. In some industries employers find it difficult to fill part-time vacancies and it is an employee's market. Value your skills and be willing to suggest negotiating pay and conditions upwards in your favour!

Agencies

Agencies are a very good source of part-time jobs and agencies of this type have grown considerably over recent years. They bridge a gap between employers who have a regular requirement for part-time help and employees who only wish to work part-time. They are in many ways the modern equivalent of overtime, whereby employers can obtain extra labour without high overtime costs or the expenses of employing their own full- or part-time staff. This has provided a wide range of choices for the employee and, in many ways, it has become a buyer's market so far as the employee is concerned, offering many opportunities to pick and choose.

Agencies include major national names such as Manpower, Kelly and ECCO and regional and local companies. Some agencies operate only in certain areas of work, whereas others operate in all areas.

Here are some tips on making a success of working part time with agencies:

■ Choose the right type of agency. Most agencies for part-time or temporary workers specialise in some particular type of work, such as catering staff, office staff or drivers.

■ Be selective. Interview your agency. Ask what they can offer you. Can they offer you as much work as you want to do? Can they offer you what might be termed desirable assignments. For example, day-time work rather than nights, or long contracts where you can settle in rather than a series of short-term assignments.

■ Look for jobs that use your skills to the fullest, and offer opportunities to develop those skills.

■ Be ready to negotiate on pay. Agencies make a profit by charging the employer much more than they pay you. They are often prepared to increase the pay they offer, especially in the case of difficult to fill positions.

- Find out what your commitments are. How much notice do you have to give? Are you able to work for someone else? Usually this is permitted, but do check.
- Find out the identity of your employer. Is it the agency or the end client? Who is responsible for paying wages and granting other benefits.
- Find out what state benefits or tax concessions you may be entitled to, depending on the country and current government policy at the end.

Other sources

The part-time jobs market is characterised by a certain amount of haphazardness. A proportion of jobs are not advertised using mainstream methods such as press advertising and agencies and, in fact, may not be advertised at all. It is important to do your own research and be persistent in order to access the full range of part-time vacancies. Less conventional methods, such as window cards or 'factory-gate' type announcements are sources which should be used. This reflects the lower status some employers attach to part-time work. Some jobs can also be had by making a direct approach to employers (i.e. unadvertised vacancies) as discussed earlier in this book.

What the employer expects

When taking up part-time employment it is useful to consider what the employer expects from part-time workers. It may, in fact, be advisable to check these expectations before accepting a post, for example:

- Flexibility. This is often an employer's main motivation for recruiting part-time workers. You may be expected to work extra/fewer hours than originally agreed.
- Loyalty. Employers normally expect the same loyalty from part-timers as full-time employees. This may cause difficulties if you wish to take other employment as well.
- Integration. In some cases, in the past, part-time employers have stood as a race apart from other employees. This attitude is becoming increasingly unacceptable and part-time employees are expected to integrate and, where appropriate, contribute to the team effort. Adopting this approach will also generally be more rewarding for the employee too.

Jobsharing: what it is and how it works

Jobsharing is a system where two or more people share one job. Normally this is achieved by each person working for several days per week, or for part of each working day, perhaps with an overlapping period during which the jobsharers can exchange information. Originally jobsharing was conceived as a way of encouraging those who could not commit to a full-time job to return to the workforce. However, employers have now come to recognise that there are practical benefits too. It allows skills to be pooled, makes recruiting easier in types of work where there are skill shortages and can also be more cost effective.

Jobsharing is an alternative worth considering if you do not wish or are unable to commit to full-time working. Although some jobs are promoted as being suitable for jobshare, employers are sometimes interested in considering this arrangement for other jobs too.

Here are some tips:

- If you are interested in or willing to jobshare always mention this in your application. It can give your application an advantage and is not considered a second-best by progressive employers.
- Focus on jobs that are most often offered for jobshare. Jobs with local authorities and public bodies often fit into this category.
- Make the match for the employer! If you have a friend or colleague interested in jobsharing then make your applications together and suggest each other as jobsharers.
- Be aware of the disadvantages of jobsharing, for example lack of continuity, difficulty of providing cover for holidays and illness, and difficulty for those you deal with in your job.
- Stress the advantages of jobsharing to the employer, such as greater flexibility and a wider range of skills from which to benefit.
- Recognise that jobsharing is a flexible arrangement and look for ways to make it even more flexible. You can jobshare 50–50, 40–60, 30–70 and so on. You can even jobshare a part-time job.

Percentage time working

Percentage time working is an arrangement where an employer and employee arrange for a job to be worked for a certain percentage of regular working hours. This might be, for example, 90 per cent, or 80 per cent or 60 per cent, or some other figure. This type of arrangement is currently little used but is likely to become more common in future as more employers and employees begin to realise the flexibility that percentage time working offers.

An inherent difference exists between part-time working and percentage time working. A part-time worker normally works fixed hours, variable at the discretion of the employer. A percentage worker, on the other hand, normally works variable hours, varied at their choice. So, for example, many percentage time workers are able to select what percentage of full-time hours they will work each week or each month. Percentage time working can therefore be an option that is particularly attractive to the employee. Some points to consider include:

- Percentage time working arrangements are of particular benefit to those with family commitments.

- Few percentage time working jobs are advertised through the usual channels. You may have to do some research to find them.

- If percentage time working might suit you, suggest it to the employer. Few employers think of suggesting it to their personnel but may be willing to consider it because of the flexibility it affords them.

- Set realistic working hours necessary to complete your duties. Clearly it is difficult to complete the workload of a full working week (for example, 40 hours) in 60 per cent percentage time working. Beware of committing yourself to unreasonable arrangements.

- Check what the arrangements are for increasing or decreasing your working hours. For example, you may be required to give one week's notice, or one month's notice.

- Team working skills are often necessary to make a success of percentage time working. (Someone else will almost certainly have to handle your duties when you are not there and you must be able to work effectively with them.)

Case study: Michelle converts to jobsharing

When Michelle Conway became pregnant she was concerned that she might have to leave her job as an Accounts Manager. Since her work involved long hours and out-of-hours work she felt she would be unable to balance both responsibilities. A friend of Michelle's suggested jobsharing, primarily as a way of re-entering the jobs market after her baby was born. Rather than leaving her current job and seeking new employment Michelle took the bold step of asking her current employer to consider jobsharing her post. They responded well to the idea and a new employee was appointed to share the post on a 50–50 basis with Michelle. The arrangement remains flexible, with Michelle's colleague increasing her hours worked to accommodate Michelle's family responsibilities, and Michelle increasing the hours she works to cover for her colleague's holidays and other periods of absence. Result: Michelle has been able to continue her career and maintain her position within the company.

Summary

■ The part-time jobs market is changing, and becoming a viable alternative to full-time working, not just a second best option.

■ When part-time working, aim to exploit the opportunities on offer and enable them to bring positive benefits to your career.

■ Consider innovative variations on part-time working, such as job sharing and percentage time working.

10 WINNING IN THE CONTRACT WORK MARKET

Contract work is becoming an increasingly common trend in the jobs market. It describes a situation whereby employees are hired on fixed-term contracts, for example, three months or a year, rather than being offered a job for an indefinite period as was traditionally the case.

The popularity of contract work has largely been employer-driven. For employers, it is an effective way of tailoring their workforce to fluctuations in their business, reducing their commitments and thus reducing their management problems and costs. In the past, contract working has been unappealing to many employees who have regarded it as a very insecure way of earning a living. The aim of this chapter, however, is to explain how to make a success of this type of working and, in particular, how to build a successful career through a series of contract jobs.

The following are some of the pros and cons of contract working.

Pros:

■ Rates of pay are often higher when compared on an hour-by-hour basis with full-time contracts, so as to compensate employees for the reduced element of security.

■ You can sometimes name your own price. Standard rates of pay do not necessarily apply to contract positions. For some contract arrangements you may be paid a lump sum which often exceeds the comparable weekly wage or monthly salary.

■ Greater flexibility. The terms and conditions are likely to be more flexible. For example, you may be able to set your own working hours or complete the job as you see fit rather than having to work to a concrete schedule. You can often name your own terms.

Cons:

■ It is inherently insecure. By definition, a contract only lasts for a limited period. When it ends there is no guarantee that it will be renewed or that you will be able to find another contract.

■ There is the extra difficulty of having to renew, negotiate or seek new contracts at the end of this period.

■ It may not be possible to arrange consecutive contracts. This may involve you in periods of unemployment, the cost of which has to be subsidised by the income from each contract you work.

Making a success of contract work

Here are a few points which can help you make a success of contract working, rather than letting it become a second-best alternative to more traditional, permanent employment:

■ You should not only accept the uncertainty of contract working, but you must actually exploit it. Look for contracts which offer a higher level of remuneration, or better opportunities than a traditional, indefinite contract might have offered. Treat it as an opportunity, and exploit every opportunity.

■ You should be ready to accept greater responsibility when contract working. For example, you may have to provide tools and equipment. You may also have to become responsible for your own training and career development.

■ You must charge more for your services, to account for the extra responsibility and also for any periods you are out of work. This is not usually a problem since employers are normally prepared to pay contract workers more than other employees, often substantially more.

■ You must put yourself and your interests first. You owe less loyalty to your employer simply because they owe less loyalty to you. Should a conflict of interests arise between doing what is best for the employer and doing what is best for you, you should normally choose the latter option.

■ Go back to working on a traditional, indefinite contract if this type of working turns out to suit you better.

Is contract work for you?

This type of working could be for you if you can accept the following implications of contract working:

■ You need to be able to accept the uncertainty of not having indefinite employment.

- You should have some sort of financial cushion to fall back on if you are between contracts. At least six month's salary is recommended.
- You should possess (or be willing to acquire) a skill that is currently in demand, thus making your services in demand.
- You may need to be mobile. It is best if you are willing to move to other parts of the country to pursue opportunities. You need to live where your customers live.
- You need to be willing to invest time and money in updating your skills and retraining. Unlike the case of indefinite employment, you won't usually find that your employer is responsible for this.
- You need to be willing to take responsibility for things that are normally handled by your employer. For example, taxation affairs, insurance.

Where to find contract jobs

To make a success of contract working you generally need to be much more flexible about finding jobs. They are not only available from the traditional sources, such as press advertising, but many others also.

Advertised jobs

Contract jobs are advertised in all the usual magazines and newspapers but may be advertised as ordinary vacancies. Approach the employer and suggest that they hire you on a contract basis. Contracts may also be promoted in the 'Contracts and Tenders' and 'Business Opportunities' sections, not just the 'Situations Vacant' sections.

Agencies

Contract jobs are handled by the usual employment agencies. Apply for any vacancies they advertise and also circulate your details to suitable agencies. When applying for a contract job through an agency it is important to establish that you are in fact applying for a contract job. In some cases although you may be working on a contract basis for an employer, the agency may be your employer. In this case you should regard yourself as an employee, with the same rights and responsibilities as employees, and not a contract worker as such.

Direct approaches to employers

A direct approach to an employer (or clients as they should be regarded) is one of the best ways of obtaining contract work. Doing this allows you to obtain work on your own terms, rather than the employers'. It also makes it easier to adjust your workload and your way of working to the most efficient and cost-effective combination.

When making an approach offering to contract work you should see your relationship as a supplier–client one rather than employee–employer. In other words, you are not working for the client but providing them with a service (your labour). As such you are offering them something they need – a professional service – rather than them offering you something you need, in terms of a job.

Action plan

Here is an action plan for getting contract work:

■ Define your talents. Decide what your speciality is going to be as a contract worker. It is better to focus on something that you are particularly good at, rather than being a so-called jack of all trades.

■ Decide on concrete reasons why employers will want to use your talents. Are you a real specialist in your field? Do you have a proven track record of success?

■ Collect evidence of your experience in your speciality. This will help you convince the client that they need to hire you. Document past projects that have been successfully completed and collect references from past employers.

■ Set up a system for gathering the names and addresses of present employers and future employers. Obtain names and addresses from trade directories, newspapers and other sources.

■ Decide how you are going to approach people. Methods to consider include press advertising, direct mail and personal contacts.

■ Approach potential employers. When you do this remember that the relationship between contract worker and employer is more like that between supplier and client, rather than employee and employer.

What the employer expects

The following are the key expectations of an employer when they retain the services of a contract worker. They are all areas which are not usually the responsibility of employees on indefinite contracts:

■ Flexibility. You may be expected to be flexible, working whatever hours are necessary to complete your task.

■ Executive responsibility. You will normally be expected to make minor decisions on your own, rather than referring them to the employer.

■ Responsibility for statutory procedures. You may find that you are responsible for dealing with matters such as tax, insurance and compliance with health and safety regulations.

Devising a career plan when contract working

When working as a contract worker you will usually find that you have greater responsibility for your career than would usually be the case. For example, while an employer employing an employee on an indefinite contract may take responsibility for training and retraining, career reviews and periodic career assessments this is not always the case with contract employees. It is important to take responsibility for your own career, ensuring that you have access to the same opportunities for advancement as other employees. Here is a checklist of pointers you should bear in mind:

■ Review the progress of your career from time to time. Look at what type of work you are doing, and the remuneration you are earning. Think about where you are on the career ladder.

■ Compare the development of your career with those on indefinite contracts. Do some research. Find out what levels of pay and conditions apply to other employees doing the same type of work. Do yours compare favourably?

■ Join professional organisations and societies. They can help keep you in touch with current practice and thinking in your trade or profession.

■ Make contact or keep in touch with other people contract working in the same industry. They can help you keep in touch with industry news, and market rates of pay and conditions.

■ Review your level of skill and training from time to time, at least annually. How does it compare? Does it need updating?

■ Keep informed about the current range of qualifications available in your trade or profession. Are there new qualifications available which you could study for? Are certain qualifications about to be made mandatory for your trade and profession?

■ Take advantage of opportunities for information interchange and development, for example, training courses, conferences, meetings and seminars. Make time for these events, no matter how busy your schedule.

Rights and responsibilities of contract workers

For the purposes of the law contract workers are normally regarded as self-employed and are therefore small businesses rather than employees. These are the main rights and responsibilities which you may have and which you should bear in mind:

■ You may be responsible for own taxation affairs. Your employer may pay you without deducting income tax. You may be responsible for filing your own income tax return with the tax authorities and paying your own income tax.

■ You may be responsible for paying your own social security or health insurance contributions, rather than relying on your employer to do this.

■ You may be responsible for providing your own professional and public liability insurance.

■ You may be responsible for any debts that you incur in the course of your trade or profession. For example, for any debts that you accrue with suppliers or others that you employ.

■ Your rights are whatever those you set down in your contract with your employer. So, if properly constructed, these can actually be greater than those which employees benefit from. For example, if you incorporate a six-month notice period into your contract and this is accepted by your client you will benefit from a more generous period of notice than is normally afforded to employees on an indefinite contract.

EXERCISES

1 Decide what might be the advantages and disadvantages of contract working for your particular job or career.

2 Consider how you might be able to take advantage of contract working opportunities in your particular job or career.

Case study: Barrie makes a success of flexible contract working

When Barrie Johnson was made redundant as a maintenance electrician at a large factory he found it very difficult to find similar employment. Few vacancies ever arose, and those that did offered much less than his previous rate of pay. While talking to a friend he heard about another company that employed maintenance electricians on a contract basis, rather than offering indefinite employment. Barrie applied for one of the contracts, which he secured, and was offered a 24-month contract to provide electrical maintenance services. Barrie was required to provide his own tools and equipment, his own liability insurance and was also required to be on call on a round-the-clock basis. To compensate, however, Barrie found that the monthly remuneration was actually 40 per cent more than his previous salary and, even after the additional costs of contract working – and the inherent insecurity – he was still substantially better off.

Summary

- Contract working (employment on a contract of limited duration) is becoming more common.
- Contract working can be advantageous to the employee, if properly set up.
- Don't neglect the need for career planning and career development when contract working.
- Be aware of your special rights and responsibilities.

11 | WINNING WITH SELF-EMPLOYMENT

Self-employment has not traditionally been considered as a direct alternative to employment. However, in the modern jobs market it has come to be accepted as one of the range of choices available to the employee wishing to succeed. This is due to the demand for greater flexibility amongst the workforce and the tend for contracting out, which has been considered in the previous chapter. It has also become an attractive option amongst many employees who regard it as a tool which they themselves can use to become more flexible and more competitive, and also to increase their earnings above those possible from direct employment.

In truth, of course, self-employment is very different to other types of employment. It is, in effect, owning and running a business, following very much the same principles as the largest corporation or conglomerate, only on a much smaller scale. Nevertheless the fact remains that self-employment is well established and proven as a way of earning a living and it is certainly a viable alternative for anyone seeking to win in the jobs market.

Is self-employment for you?

Self-employment is best entered into if you feel you want to exploit the opportunities that it offers, rather than because you feel you have been forced into it. Taking self-employment because, for example, you cannot get a job elsewhere is rarely a good idea.

Here are some pros and cons of self-employment

Pros:

■ Self-employment offers flexibility, to work as and when you like, as much or as little as you like, and to do what you like.

■ It is easier to keep up with trends and changes. If you see better opportunities in a different type of work, or in another area, then it is much easier to move on and exploit them. Levels of self-employment are particularly high in sunrise industries.

■ It is a more competitive way of selling yourself. Normally a self-employed person goes out and looks for opportunities to exploit, rather than wait for jobs to apply for. Self-employment gives you the flexibility to do this.

■ It allows you freedom to organise your career around other aspects of your life. For example, if you prefer to work in the evenings or weekends, or part time, then you can.

■ It is usually better paid and offers other financial benefits. Self-employed people normally earn more than employed people doing the same job, once all pay and benefits are taken into account. This may be because there is more incentive to work when you work for yourself, or simply because it is a more efficient way of earning. It should not be taken for granted, however, as some self-employed people earn no more, although few earn much less than an employed person doing the same job.

■ It offers extra challenges which you may not be able to enjoy in employment.

■ It has future prospects. The self-employed and small business sector is growing. These types of enterprise are becoming a larger force in the economy, while many large corporations are downsizing.

Cons:

■ It can be very hard work, especially for owner-operator businesses with no staff to share the workload.

■ It can be very uncertain. There is no way of guaranteeing a regular workload, nor a regular income.

■ It may call for skills which you do not have. For example, financial and marketing skills.

■ It may result in you having to run a business, which you may not wish to do.

■ It is not an automatic route to higher income. Your income is directly linked to your personal input.

■ It may take time and money to build your business up to a productive level.

Self-Employment could be for you if:

■ You have skills and talents which are in demand, or are willing to learn them.

■ You are open to learning new skills, especially those connected with business management, if you do not have them.

■ You are willing to take a risk. In this regard it is not just willingness to take a risk that is important. It is best if you can afford to take that risk also.

■ You are ready to exploit the opportunities.

■ You find it difficult to commit to regular working hours and would, for example, find the ability to work in the evenings and weekends useful. This might apply if you have family responsibilities. It does not, however, mean that you do not need to consider yourself a suitable candidate for self-employment in all other ways.

Self-employment may not be for you if:

■ You lack experience in your current job, and feel that you still have skills that you need to develop.

■ You are not confident about selling yourself. All self-employment involves selling to some extent.

■ You like to work regular hours, and take regular holidays. Few self-employed people can afford these 'luxuries', certainly not in the early years.

■ You have little, or insufficient, capital to invest in your business.

In summary, people who do best from self-employment are very often those who have or are being successful in employment but feel that self-employment offers more room for growth and development compared with looking for an employed position with more responsibility.

Essential preparations for self-employment

The following points comprise a checklist of areas you should explore before deciding to go ahead and become self employed:

■ You should have an idea for your business. Will you make a product? Provide a service? Run a retail business?

■ You should have valid reasons for believing that you can run this business as well or better than anyone else. Ask yourself why customers should come to you.

■ You should feel sure that you have a market for your product or service.

■ You should have found a source of supply of your product or basic requirements to provide your service.

■ You should know what the costs are likely to be of setting up your project, including such costs as premises, stock, staff and working capital.

■ You should feel sure that you will be able to sell your product or service at a competitive price. A good rule of thumb is that you should be able to charge less than your nearest competitors.

■ You should know how you will reach your customers. Are they personal contacts of yours? Will you need to advertise? In the press? On television? Using mailshots?

■ You should have a very good idea of who your potential customers are. If you know exactly who these people or companies will be then so much the better. If possible, sound them out about doing business with you – ask them if they will be prepared to do business with you.

■ You have the money available to set up the idea, or know where you will be able to obtain it, for example, a loan or grant.

If you do not have all of this information then self-employment may not be for you, or you may be better delaying taking up the opportunity until you have this information.

Setting up your self-employment project

Self-employment is essentially setting up a business and there is always much to be done before you can begin trading. Here are the main areas you cover when setting up your project:

■ Have a target launch date. This gives you something to work towards. That said, you do not have to start on one day. Many people who become self-employed enter self-employment on a gradual basis, perhaps starting with just one or two initial products and then introducing more, or even starting on a part-time basis.

Look into financing. Assess what personal capital you have available. See what loans or grants might be available, and ascertain if you are eligible for them.

Arrange for an initial source of stock and supplies. Try to locate and select suppliers who can offer a regular supply and stable supplies for several months hence, thus making planning and budgeting easier.

Sound out your likely customers. Will they buy from you? How much and at what price?

■ Obtain suitable premises. Try to choose premises which will allow for the growth of the business at least 24 months hence.

■ Decide on equipment required and purchasing. Look into financing options, such as rental or leasing.

■ Decide on staff required, if any. Self-employment businesses are owner-operator concerns but, equally, some employ others. If staff are required recruitment of suitable personnel should be started well in advance.

■ Look into statutory requirements such as tax and VAT. Hire an accountant if necessary.

■ Look into legal problems. Are there legal problems associated with your type of business? Are any licences required? If so, resolve these issues before making a commitment to proceed.

■ Organise an initial advertising campaign. If you are starting from scratch then you may have to do more advertising, at a greater cost, than you might have envisaged.

Tips to make self-employment more successful

The following pointers will provide an insight into how to make a success of self-employment:

■ Start from the point of view of success, rather than failure. If you have become self-employed because, for example, you have been made redundant then always tell others that you have started your own business to take advantage of the greater opportunities.

■ Choose something that other people have commented favourably on as the basis for your project. If people have said that you are an excellent cook, writer or mechanic then these are skills you should exploit in your business.

■ Be objective. Look at what you are doing from an independent standpoint. Ask yourself would you do business with your business?

■ Take a long look at what you are selling and for how much. Ask yourself, why should customers buy from you? What are you going to do to make them an offer they can't refuse?

■ Divide your time effectively between the different functions a small business has to do, such as sales, production, customer service and accounts. Don't just concentrate on what you like doing. If necessary, make yourself tackle the things you don't like doing.

■ Be ready to acquire new skills. Attend courses and seminars on, for example, selling or bookkeeping.

■ Allow for the fact that it may take longer to set up than you imagine.

■ Be ready to change direction. If your original project doesn't work as well as you thought be prepared to consider changing it in some way.

■ Be ready to work longer and/or irregular hours – at all times, not just when you first start up. Few self-employed people work nine-to-five.

■ Be prepared to charge more than you expect. Remember that as well as paying yourself you have to cover your expenses and make a profit too. So, whereas, for example, you might be perfectly happy to earn £25,000 as an employee you might need to turn over £50,000 or more as a self-employed person to end up with the same or better personal earnings. (This is just to illustrate the point, the actual sum may be more or may be much less.)

■ Periodically review your operations and your income to ensure that you are making a good return in comparison to people who are working as employees in the same industry. If they are doing better than you, should you go back to being an employee? Remember, self-employment is there to be used as a tool for your own benefit. It is not there to benefit other people.

How to avoid self-employment pitfalls

Although self-employment is often made out to be a road to riches there are also pitfalls which are best avoided with the benefit of advance information. While some people become very rich by breaking the chains of paid employment and becoming self-employed most people do not. There are, however, hundreds of thousands of people making a comfortable income from self-employment. The following will help you to avoid the usual pitfalls:

Avoid going self-employed if it is your only option.

Don't try to copy someone else's success story. It is rarely as simple as that, and you won't find out until you start up.

■ Be wary about buying business packages and franchises that set you up in business. Often, the person selling the package makes the most from them. Franchises are often most suitable for people who already have some business experience.

■ Spend the minimum possible on setting up the business. Make do with second hand machinery and equipment if you can. This will release your funds for more pressing uses.

■ Keep operating costs as low as possible. For example, if you can practically work from home then do so.

■ Underestimate your market. Realise that a lot of the advertising you do won't pay off initially, and a lot of the orders you are promised won't materialise.

■ Don't offer to work for too little, just to get in enough business to keep you going.

■ Remember the extra responsibilities. You are responsible for collecting and paying your own income tax and VAT. You may have responsibilities to your staff. You also have other legal commitments such as, if a sole trader, responsibilities for any debts that you incur in your business.

EXERCISES

1 Consider whether or not your particular job or career might be suitable for converting to a self-employed basis.

2 List what the advantages might be of doing this.

3 List what the disadvantages might be of doing this.

Case studies:
A self-employment success story

Jean worked as an accountant for a small engineering company. She frequently received requests from other small businesses locally who asked for her help with their accounts in the evenings and at weekends. Jean worked out that she could probably earn as much from her part-time assignments as her full-time job. She decided to leave and set up her own accountancy practice. Before doing so she asked her current boss if he would be willing for her to continue to work on his accounts on a self-employed basis. He agreed and Jean started her new business with three customers signed up to use it. Result: Jean has doubled her income without working longer hours. Reasons: she had an in-demand skill and sounded out possible customers before she left her previous job.

When self-employment may not be the solution

Martin worked as a mechanic in a motor workshop. When the garage lost several major accounts Martin knew that he was likely to be made redundant. He decided to 'jump before he was pushed' and left. He decided to make a complete break with the past and bought a small franchise which involved selling chemicals to the motor trade on a van sales round operation. After six months in business Martin's venture wasn't even breaking even. Martin decided to close it down and took a mechanic's job with a nearby garage. Result: Martin became completely disillusioned with self-employment. Reasons: Martin went self-employed for the wrong reasons, as a solution to redundancy rather than because he wanted to exploit the opportunities on offer. He didn't capitalise on his existing skills and, additionally, didn't give his new venture sufficient time to become successful.

Summary

■ Self-employment is becoming an increasingly valid way of winning in the jobs market.

■ Only go self-employed for the right reasons.

■ Plan the preparation and setting up of your business carefully. Much more is involved than any form of employment.

■ Be ready to change. Self-employment calls for extreme flexibility.

12 | WINNING IN THE WORLDWIDE JOBS MARKET

This chapter looks at how to find and choose jobs abroad, thus expanding your choice from several thousands of vacancies in your own area to, potentially, millions of vacancies worldwide!

Is working abroad for you?

Working abroad has become an increasingly popular option within the last 20 years or so. From the employee's point of view this widens your choice enormously, from only those job vacancies available in your own country to many, many more available worldwide. For example, the workforce of Europe alone is reckoned to be around 120 million. The workforce of the world is unknown, but is likely to be several hundred times more! While all these jobs aren't available to those from other countries a good many of them are and, as a job seeker, it widens your choice vastly.

Here are some pros and cons of working abroad.

Pros:

■ Higher pay is offered in some countries.

■ More choice of vacancies. Some countries have a shortage of certain types of personnel. In these cases very high pay is likely to be offered.

■ Greater responsibility and prestige is attached to certain types of work in other countries.

■ Better way of life. You may be able to find a country which you think offers a better way of life. For example, more opportunities, better social life, better weather.

Cons:

■ There are usually restrictions on foreigners travelling to other countries to look for and take up work.

■ It can be hard to find work, when you do not have a knowledge of the employment scene in that particular country.

■ Standards and qualifications may differ considerably. Your qualifications might not be accepted at all, or you may have to retrain.

■ The way of life is not always an improvement, once advantages and disadvantages are balanced out.

Important considerations

Here are some important considerations you need to bear in mind when you are thinking about going to work in another country.

■ It is usually necessary to speak the local language, both to find a job and to carry it out. With some exceptions, employers won't normally employ you unless you have a good knowledge of the local language.

■ You must check that your qualifications are acceptable in the country in which you wish to work. Even if they are you may need to have them formally adopted by a professional organisation in the relevant country. This can take some time.

■ You must check immigration restrictions. An offer of a job does not guarantee you a visa and/or work or residence permit in most countries. In some countries, you won't be granted permission to live there unless you have been offered a job. You can become caught up in a vicious circle!

■ Sample the way of life if at all possible. Working in a foreign country is not the same as taking a holiday there. It is a good idea to spend some time there before making the final decision.

How to find a job abroad

Finding a job very much involves a proactive approach. Rarely are foreign jobs offered by chance. In fact, most employers tend to assume that their employees do not want to move abroad. You will, therefore, need to go out and actively look for a job abroad.

As a first step, explore what opportunities there might be for working abroad with your current employer. Make it clear to those with whom you come into contact that you are interested in a position abroad. If your present employer has branches or subsidiaries abroad then talk to your personnel officer about it, or ask to be given an introduction. Unless you take such steps you are very unlikely to be offered a position. Also explore the options for work experience, placements and exchange schemes abroad.

If none of these methods are suitable then here are some other methods you can use to find a suitable job abroad:

Using employment agencies

A number of employment agencies offer jobs abroad or, alternatively, recruit workers from abroad. You can find out about these by using the 'Yellow Pages' directory available at the library. Try both agencies in your own country, and those in the country in which you wish to work. It is important to choose carefully, since agencies normally specialise in different industries and may not handle all types of jobs. Agencies of this type can normally only help those who have some experience of a particular type of work.

In many countries it is also possible for those from abroad to use the national employment service in order to find a job. To do this, however, you may have to speak the local language well. In some countries, private employment agencies are forbidden by law and you may have to use the national employment service as there is no alternative.

Here are some points to remember:

- Build your own address book of agencies and keep adding to it.
- Send each agency a copy of your CV, together with a covering letter telling them what type of job you are looking for and in which areas you wish to work.
- If they charge a fee, obtain full details of what this will be. Normally employment agencies are paid by the employer rather than the employee. However, some agencies may charge either a flat fee or a proportion of your future salary.
- Normally you can register with as many agencies as you like. Indeed, you should register with as many as possible in order to get the best choice of jobs.

Using newspapers and journals

Newspapers and professional journals are a good source of vacancies abroad. However, you will not usually find that any one newspaper or journal contains a very wide selection. Therefore, you will need to locate and read as many suitable publications as possible and read them on a regular basis in order to get a good selection of vacancies. Set up a system for obtaining and reviewing these vacancies, on the following basis:

■ National newspapers offer the best choice of vacancies abroad. Regional and local newspapers have little if any to choose from.

■ Professional journals can be a good source of vacancies, if there is one for your particular trade or profession.

■ Use foreign newspapers and journals. Find out about these at your local library. It is usually possible to subscribe to foreign newspapers and journals, although the cost may be high. Foreign embassies and consulates sometimes have reading rooms where you can consult their relevant national newspapers free of charge.

■ When using foreign publications remember the time delay. You need to prepare and submit your application quickly, or it may be too late. Telephone or fax your application wherever possible.

■ Make use of the Internet. Some foreign newspapers publish websites, so that you can gain access to vacancies on the day of publication rather than waiting.

The direct approach: approaching the employers

Making direct approaches to employers can be a very successful way of finding a job abroad. It helps to solve the problem of actually finding out foreign vacancies, which can be difficult when long distances are involved. Also, in many cases, employers are willing to consider workers from abroad (or even need them) but have very little knowledge of recruiting in that particular country. Therefore, do the following:

■ Build up a hit list, of potential employers in the industry or country in which you wish to work. For example, if you wish to work in the petrochemicals industry compile a list of petrochemical companies. This should include companies based in the country concerned, as well as companies based in your own or other countries who have operations in the country concerned.

■ Use all possible sources of information. Look in the 'Yellow Pages' and all relevant trade directories. Ask at your library for these. The Chamber of Commerce for the relevant country can often provide you with a list of companies. Also make use of the Internet.

- Make speculative applications to all likely potential employers. Send them a copy of your CV with a covering letter introducing yourself.
- Be prepared to be persistent using this method. You may need to contact a large number of prospective employers in order to find a job that is suitable for you.

How to apply for a job abroad

The following pointers will help you when you locate suitable vacancies and are ready to apply for a job abroad:

- Apply as soon as possible. Delays in communications using foreign postal systems, and also time differences, can put you at a disadvantage compared with other applicants.
- Telephone regarding the application if at all possible. This will help you make sure that the job is really suitable and also find out other clues that may be helpful in applying for it.
- If you are invited for interview find out if the employer will cover the costs. Some companies will, although you should not assume that they will.
- Find out if your qualifications are accepted in the relevant foreign country. Sometimes they are, but more usually they are not. In some cases they may have to be officially recertified by a professional organisation, or you may have to undertake some retraining.
- Find out what the language requirements are. What languages will you need to speak, and to what level?
- If you are offered a job find out exactly what the terms and conditions are before accepting it. Is it an indefinite or a fixed-term contract? Fixed-term contracts are much more usual for expatriate workers. What pay is being offered? It may not necessarily be any higher because you are an expatriate worker. Are there any other fringe benefits? Benefits such as free or subsidised accommodation, relocation expenses and free flights home are sometimes offered to expatriate workers, but you should not assume so.

Practical considerations for expatriates

Here are some of the main practical considerations you should take into account when going to live and work abroad:

- *Tax*. In which country will your income be taxed? As tax rates and conditions vary considerably around the world this can make a great difference to the amount of your income that you have to give up in tax. Normally you remain liable to the tax system in your country of origin unless and until you spend a substantial proportion of the tax year abroad. If you return home too often then this might make you liable to tax in your country of origin.

- *Social security*. Are you required to contribute to a social security system in either your country of origin or the country you will be living and working in. Often it is advisable to keep paying into the system in your country of origin so that you remain entitled to benefits. If necessary, take expert advice on tax, social security and other aspects of financial planning.

- *Health insurance*. Remember that most countries do not provide free healthcare as a matter of course. You may have to take out private health insurance to cover for the costs of this. In many countries your employer may provide this as a fringe benefit but you should check to make sure as, otherwise, the costs can be high.

- *Housing*. The costs of housing can vary considerably around the world. It may be much cheaper, or much more expensive than you are used to. In some countries there may even be a shortage of suitable accommodation. Check costs and availability in advance.

- *Your partner and children*. How do your partner and children, if any, feel about the prospect of living abroad? Are there facilities for them, or would they prefer to stay at home? Are there employment opportunities for your partner, or not? In most countries, they may find it difficult to get a suitable job. What sort of schools are available for your children? What language is spoken and what costs are involved? Remember that international schools are only available in a few areas and the costs of private education can be high.

Work permit and visa requirements

When living and working abroad it is important to check what work permits and visas may be required. In many countries where a permit and visa is not required for a tourist visit, one is required when you are working. Being offered a job does not automatically mean that you will be granted a work permit and visa.

■ Always assume you will need a work permit and visa when working abroad. There are very few countries where this is not necessary. One of the few exceptions is for European Union (EU) nationals who do not need a work permit or visa to work in any other EU country.

■ In many cases work permits are only granted where there is no suitable national of the country who can do the job.

■ Always make your own enquiries. In most cases foreign employers are not experts on immigration policy. In some cases they may not even be able to help you with the application. Make enquiries with the relevant embassy or consulate about what procedure to follow.

■ Apply well in advance. It can take several weeks or months for a work permit or visa to be granted.

■ Check to see if you also need a residence permit, both for yourself and accompanying family members. Even EU nationals going to work in another EU country require a residence permit, which can be obtained on arrival.

EXERCISES

1 Consider what the advantages and disadvantages might be of working abroad for your particular job or career.

2 Make a list of sources of jobs abroad that you might use.

3 Consider what the differences might be between applying for a job in your own country and applying for a job abroad.

Case study: Anna makes the move to a job abroad

Anna Holmes was a nurse and decided that she would like to work abroad for a year or two, with a view to moving permanently in the future. She read the professional journal *Nursing Times* regularly, but discovered that the number of advertisements for working in the countries she preferred (such as Australia and Canada) were few.

Anna spent half a day at her local library reading the Australian and Canadian 'Yellow Pages' looking for agencies which handled nursing assignments. She sent a copy of her CV and a covering letter to about 30 agencies, several of whom offered her contract jobs of between six and twelve months.

Anna did some research with the relevant consulates and professional associations. She found that it was necessary to have her nursing qualifications recertified in the country in which she wished to work. She applied well in advance, not giving notice from her current post until authorisation had been granted.

Anna started work on a six-month nursing contract in Australia and at the time of writing has discovered that she is eligible to emigrate there permanently if she wishes.

Summary

- Working abroad will become an increasingly viable option for those wanting to win in the jobs market.

- Consider the pros and cons carefully. While there are many attractions to living and working abroad, there are also many drawbacks. It is important to try and avoid the 'grass is always greener on the other side' syndrome!

- Make use of all the possible sources of jobs abroad, in order to obtain a good selection.

- Bear in mind the practical considerations when making your choice, such as tax, health and provision for your family.

FINAL ADVICE

In this book we've tried to bring you every possible technique and idea to help you win in the job market. The rest is up to you. Only you can apply these techniques and ideas and make them succeed.

In the past it *might* have been possible to leave things to chance. In the past people did, indeed, achieve well paid and responsible positions simply by working hard. This is rarely the situation today. In such a competitive, fast moving market place, with so many changes taking place, no wise job seeker can afford to do this anymore. You wouldn't leave an important meeting or even a social engagement entirely to chance, so why your career?

If all this seems daunting, don't be deterred. You don't have to use every method we've discussed. Just a handful of tips from this book, used wisely really can help you get where you want to be. They can help you get that new job, or your first job, or get that promotion, change your career completely or even work abroad if that is what you want.

Try to take a systematic approach. Review your career at regular intervals - monthly or quarterly – look at what progress you have made, and decide what tips and techniques you can employ over coming months. Over the year as a whole it *will* make all the difference to your pay, job status and current employment prospects.

Finally, if you only make use of four pieces of advice from this book, try to make use of these:

- ■ Remember that the job market is continually changing, and at a faster rate than ever before.
- ■ Realise that you need to keep up with changes in the job market, if you are to win in it.
- ■ Take a systematic approach to succeeding in your job or career. Don't leave it to chance.
- ■ Make use of all possible advantages that can help you develop your career.

INDEX